# Never Too Young to Change the World

Inspiring True Stories of Young People

## By Br. Dan O'Riordan

Copyright © 2020 by Br. Dan O'Riordan.
First paperback edition October 2020.

Cover design and book formatting by Dari Goldman.
Book editing by Br. Donnell Neary.

ISBN 9798666604489 (paperback)

# Dedication

Dedicated to all the young people written about in the pages of this book. They are one of the greatest blessings in my life and heroes to many others.

# Acknowledgements

I wish to thank all the young people who have graced my journey, many who are heroes in my life and an inspiration to all.

I am grateful to the Marist Brothers for giving me so many opportunities to serve young people in my various roles as a Brother.

I am forever indebted to so many fellow Marists who joined me on countless retreats, pilgrimages, trips and adventures including John Allen, Marcus Allen, Ed Kennedy, Pat and Maureen Hagan, Marcus O'Grady, Br. Owen Ormsby, Br. Alfred George, Br. Brian Poulin, Matt Fallon, Tim Hagan, Dan Hurley, Nick "Chachi" Rella, Jameson Mayr, Loretta Metz, Roxzann and Melissa McCulley, Jodi (Block) Williams Reager, Denny and Brenda Beiter, Paul Franco, Carl Semmler, Marty Wingert, Jeff Gallagher and Tomas O'Riordan.

I would like to acknowledge the Redemptorist community and staff at St. Alfonso Retreat house in Long Branch, NJ for providing me the perfect retreat space to write the reflections that became this book.

I also express my sincere gratitude to Br. Donnell Neary, who edited this book, and to Dari Goldman, who designed the cover and helped with the formatting of this publication.

# Contents

"Don't let anyone look down on you because you are young, but set an example for the believers in speech, in conduct, in love, in faith and in purity."

*1 Timothy 4:12 (NIV)*

# Introduction

For more than thirty years, I have had the extraordinary privilege to spend most of my days working with young people in a variety of roles such as teacher, counselor, coach, campus minister and mentor. All of these experiences have convinced me that young people are the single greatest hope and gift we have in this world.

Unfortunately, many times in this world young people are not always valued for the people they already are nor for the potential impact they will make with the gift of their lives. Too often, members of society and many leaders in our world and church consider young people to simply be over idealistic and lacking real life experiences. I frequently wish these same leaders or critics of young people could see the world through the eyes of the very young people they rarely highlight as an important voice in our world.

In the chapters that follow, I will share many inspiring stories of amazing young people I have personally known who have significantly improved countless lives and who, at a young age, have already made a great difference in this world. Each one of these young people are witnesses to the fact that the best of humanity can be found in the hearts, lives and example of our greatest treasure, namely young people.

I was graced in my own life to have great mentors and influences who taught me the importance of recognizing the impact and potential that young people can have to be the needed change in our world for a brighter and more hope-filled future. Each of my mentors deeply believed in young people as the world's greatest potential. The fruits of their beliefs and hard work helped allow many young people to achieve their promise and become all that God had intended them to be. The two most significant mentors in my life were Br. Regis and Br. Leo. I met both of them in my freshman year of high school. They initially would serve as guidance counselors to me and eventually would become lifelong mentors and close friends.

I met Br. Regis toward the end of October of my freshman year at Archbishop Molloy High School. It was around the time of the conclusion of the first academic marking period. I received a guidance pass during homeroom and went to see him at the allotted time period. He asked me how I liked being a freshman at Archbishop Molloy. I told him I loved it and had made a lot of new friends and that I really enjoyed being part of the cross-country team. He chuckled and told me that I may not enjoy it much longer as I had just failed six out of seven classes for the first marking period and unless I turn things around, I will not be allowed to continue at Molloy after my freshman year. Within days he helped me get needed tutoring in the subjects I was failing and continued to work with me on my academics until I was able to get my grades up. He was very proud that I won the most improved student award at the end of the year. I went from having a failing average to being on the honor roll but more importantly, with his help, I gained the confidence I was lacking to succeed academically in school.

When I was in grade school and getting ready to take the Catholic high school entrance exam, my teachers asked me what three high school choices I would be listing on the exam. When I told them that I wanted to put Molloy as my first, second and third choice, they told me that I shouldn't even put Molloy down as any choice as I would never get accepted into such a rigorously academic school. I'm grateful I didn't heed their advice, but because of their doubts in my abilities, I did carry a good bit of fear and anxiety going into Molloy as to whether I would be able to meet the academic demands and challenges that I would face. Thanks to Br. Regis I quickly overcame my fears and intimidations to enjoy a solid academic career all the way through graduate school.

There were over four hundred freshmen at Molloy each year and Br. Regis was the sole freshman guidance counselor for almost forty years at the school. I came to see firsthand that he would diligently and lovingly journey with each and every freshman, assisting them in any way he could and would often remain a positive and encouraging force in their lives well beyond their high school years.

Br. Regis knew I had the potential to make it at Molloy and through his constant encouragement and motivation I was lucky enough to be one of his many success stories. Years later when I began my own teaching career, I always tried to get assigned the weakest academic math classes as I could easily relate to the struggles of so many of those students who, similar to my experience, were not necessarily poor students but often just lacked the confidence to achieve success.

Once I started to turn my academics around and improve my study and time management skills, Br. Regis introduced me to Br. Leo, who would soon become another great mentor in my life. Br. Regis told me that Br. Leo would really be able to help me grow in building up my self-confidence which I was struggling with at the time.

Br. Leo was the single greatest influence I would ever know. His office, called "The Cave," was a small dark room with all the walls covered with pictures of kids and lots of great quotes. It was a room where miracles happened on a daily basis. Br Leo had developed two incredibly impactful programs over his many years of working with young people and those programs continue to be the cornerstone of that great school.

The first was his "S.M.I.L.E." program which focused on helping all young people to learn and know "Something More in Life's Experience." This program allowed young people who might be struggling with many realities such as grief, divorce, alcoholism in their family, drug problems, anger, low self-esteem, sexuality, etc. to have a safe place to work through those issues. The unique and remarkably successful way that Br. Leo designed the program, by utilizing what he called "Likes with Likes," has impacted thousands of lives. If a young person was struggling with his parents getting a divorce, Leo had him attend an after school anonymous group that was focused on divorce. Leo would have older students, who overcame similar struggles in this area, lead the group and share their insights and stories. These groups didn't resolve the divorce or make problems go away but gave the struggling young person the coping skills necessary to get through their struggle. Once a young person worked through a particular issue then they in turn would "play it forward" by becoming a leader of a group to help future students with the same problem or issue. The first day I met Leo, he simply told me that he needed me to help others that were struggling with self-esteem and asked if I would be willing to share my story with them. Over the next four years, I witnessed many miracles happen in "The Cave" and the lives of many young people were transformed. The reason that Leo was so successful came down to two simple facts. He wholeheartedly and unconditionally loved every single young person that walked into his office and he believed firmly that each one of them was bound for greatness and could change the world. It was his job to help them come to realize it.

The second program that he developed that continues to impact many lives is the Molloy peer counselling program that is part of every sophomore's schedule. For one marking period, every sophomore is scheduled to be part of a peer group of ten sophomores, two senior peer group leaders and an adult moderator. The senior leaders are trained on how to effectively run a group and ensure participation by all group members. Confidentiality about what is said in the group is a sacred tradition of over fifty years and is well-respected. The senior leaders lead the group through a series of topics that are discussed over the course of the ten weeks including self-esteem, study habits, dating, sexuality, bullying, diversity, etc. I had the privilege to be a peer group leader during my senior year and the skills I acquired would help me many times during college when I would volunteer to work on retreats and encounters at our Marist Brothers Retreat Center in Esopus, NY.

Three other great influences on my life who similarly believed in the potential of young people to be a force for good in this world are St. Marcellin Champagnat, the founder of the Marist Brothers, Br. Roger, the founder of the Taizé community and St. Mother Teresa of Calcutta.

St Marcellin, who was born in rural France at the end of the French Revolution, had very little formal education himself. When a visiting priest to his family farm asked him if he might consider making a difference in the world as a priest, he became very intrigued by the possibility. Marcellin, who came from a very religious family, pondered the priest's invitation and decided to enter the minor seminary. He didn't last long and quickly was asked to leave for his failure to keep up with the academic requirements. His mother encouraged him not to give up on his vocation and dream and secured the help of her son-in-law, a teacher, to tutor the future saint so that he might re-enter the seminary. Marcellin eventually was ordained in 1816 and was assigned to the small farming hamlet of LaValla in the mountains of the Rhone Valley region of France. He quickly came to know the families in his parish and soon realized that there were many young people in his area that had no possibility of a future because of the lack of opportunities for such children to receive an education. He dreamed of starting an order of Religious Brothers, who would be dedicated to teaching poor and marginalized children. Within months of his arrival to LaValla, he made that dream a reality with the help of his first two recruits. Both were young and uneducated, but Marcellin saw their potential and would quickly teach them and train them to be teachers. Other young people soon joined this new adventure and the Marist Brothers became a reality. For more than 200 years now, the Marist Brothers continue to be dedicated to the Christian education and evangelization of young people, especially the least favored. Marcellin saw a need in the world in which he lived and was not afraid to trust young people to become the solution to address that need.

In 1940, Br. Roger Schütz, founded the Taizé Community, an ecumenical monastic community in the small French countryside town of Taizé, about five miles from Cluny. During the second world war, his community was successful in hiding and rescuing many refugees from the horrors of the Holocaust. When the war ended in 1945, Br. Roger believed that the only hope the world had for true reconciliation and a future was by entrusting that hope and future into the hands of young people. Br. Roger and the Brothers of Taizé opened up their community to young people as a place where they might come to pray and find reconciliation among other young people from nations that had been at war with each other. Young people enthusiastically responded to the invitation and the community of Taizé continues to be a place that draws more than one hundred thousand young people annually for retreats, prayer, spiritual direction and opportunities for service. I have been blessed to have brought many young people on pilgrimage to Taizé over the years and each time I was always in awe at the large number of young people openly living their faith and having a shared desire to help make our world a more peaceful, loving and humane one.

In the early 1990's, I had the opportunity to meet Mother Teresa of Calcutta who, apart from winning the Nobel Peace Prize, would also become a Catholic Saint. During that time period, the Marist Brothers administered Sacred Heart grade school in the south Bronx. The Brothers lived next to the school near the convent, which at the time was utilized by the Missionaries of Charity, the order founded by Mother Teresa. While she was in New York to speak at the United Nations, she decided that she would also visit her sisters at the convent at Sacred Heart. The parish of Sacred Heart arranged for Mother Teresa to speak at one of the masses during her visit, which I was lucky enough to attend. She also visited the school and spent a great deal of time speaking with the young people she met. What impressed me most about this tiny woman of immense faith was the simple but yet profound advice she shared with the young people she met. She told them that if they wanted to change the world, not to come to Calcutta, but instead change the world that they lived in. She assured them that every day of their lives they would not have to travel too far from their own front doors to encounter someone in need of their help. Sometimes it will be a stranger or homeless person, sometimes a family member or friend, but each will be an opportunity to welcome and serve that person as Christ himself. She told them that as young people they had the power to change the world and that the world needed them. She closed by saying, "Remember love is not about doing great things, but doing small things with great love."

In recent years, a number of young people have made national and world news headlines by the impact of their stories and by their commitment to bring about needed changes in our world. I will share two of the many great examples of these amazing, "now famous" young people of today who are making an incredible difference in our world.

People all around our world have become inspired by the story of Malala Yousafzai, who was the fifteen-year-old girl shot in the face by the Taliban in 2012 for attempting to attend school in her native Pakistan. She refused to allow the events of that day from stopping her pursuit of gaining an education. She went on to graduate from Oxford University with a BA. By age sixteen, she became a prominent and outspoken advocate for the education and rights of young girls in countries that forbid such possibilities. In 2014, at the age of seventeen, she became the youngest recipient in history of the Nobel Peace Prize. Time Magazine featured her on numerous occasions as one of the most influential people globally. One of the most heartwarming and inspirational speeches that I have ever watched is her 2013 address to the United Nations, which is available on YouTube.

A second recent example of another young person that is making great strides for needed change in our world is the story of Greta Thunberg. She currently is seventeen years of age and a leading environmental activist, who has gained international recognition for her efforts in fighting the crisis of climate change. She remains very outspoken against the many world leaders who do too little and in some cases even deny the impact that this worldwide crisis will have on future generations. She likewise gave a stirring speech at the United Nations during the 2019 Climate Action Summit. She became the youngest Time Person of the Year, has been listed by Time magazine as among the 100 most influential people in the world, has been included in Forbes magazine's listing of the 100 most powerful women in the world and already has been nominated twice for the Nobel Peace Prize.

The stories and witness of Malala and Greta are powerful and should serve as reminders to all of us never to underestimate the impact and potential that a young person can make in our world and that one does not need to be of any given age or hold prominent jobs, titles or offices to truly be a force for change. In the chapters that follow, I share personal stories of similar young people who have made a significant impact on our world, but whose stories will probably never be covered by the media or nominated for humanitarian awards. Their witness and inspiration are no less great.

"Do Not Follow Where The Path May Lead. Go Instead Where There Is No Path And Leave A Trail."

*– Ralph Waldo Emerson*

# 1

## Newton
## and the children of
## Alpha School and Orphanage

Jamaica, West Indies

In the summer of 1993, I traveled with three Marist Brothers and three college students on a mission trip for five weeks to work at the Alpha school and orphanage on the island of Jamaica, West Indies. Earlier that year, a hurricane had devastated much of the island and had caused serious damage to a number of the buildings on the property of the orphanage. Six of the buildings needed to have their roofs replaced. The roofs were a relatively simple design of wood with sheets of galvanized metal as covering.

We arrived on July 1st and quickly experienced extreme heat and high humidity that most of us had never known. The two older brothers stayed in a small house on the property which we would all gather in for our meals and prayer each day. Br. Todd, I and our three college volunteers shared a small makeshift room in one of the dorms. Our room had one small window, no fans and a room temperature usually above ninety-five degrees. Needless to say, sleeping was difficult and often uncomfortable.

There were 185 children living at Alpha. They ranged in age from about four up to eighteen. All the children not only went to school, but also were required to learn a trade so that they might gain employment when they graduated at the age of eighteen. There were a number of options for them to choose from in regard to learning a trade. Some would learn carpentry, others automotive work, while many would focus on learning a musical instrument. The school had a long tradition of producing a great band and many of the school's graduates went on to prominent musical careers. Most of Bob Marley's band were former Alpha Boys as was Bob Marley's own brother.

The children lived very simple lives. Each child owned two pairs of shorts, two t-shirts, a change of underwear and a toothbrush. Three times a day they received a bowl full of food. Breakfast was always oatmeal, lunch and dinner were mostly rice with some vegetables and spices added. Everyone drank water. I quickly realized the extent of their poverty as I watched a number of them play soccer on a rocky grassless field that was their soccer pitch. I was amazed at their skill level and their ability to not seem affected by the brutal heat and even more surprised to find out that the reason they were playing with a coconut was that the orphanage could not afford real soccer balls.

We actually arrived on the day of Alpha's graduation and watched as the seniors received their certificates and would move out and onto the next stage of their lives. After the ceremony, we were introduced to Newton, who had just graduated as the school's first culinary arts graduate. We were told that he would be cooking all of our dinners for us so that we would not get malnourished during our stay. To say that we ate like kings was an understatement. Our dinners were often simple but each more delicious than the previous one. Thanks to Newton, we all came to savor Jerk Fish, Jamaican beef patties and vegetable curries.

The biggest struggle I had over the first week, apart from the oppressive heat, was that I was going through caffeine withdrawal as a result of not having access to diet coke. At that time, I was very addicted to diet coke and would normally have one or two for breakfast each morning to get my biological engine running for the day ahead. By the end of the first week, I woke one morning with a bad headache and began bartering with God. I told him how I'm not complaining about getting little to no sleep due to the heat or almost getting dehydrated while working on the roofs during the hottest part of the day but I wondered if having a simple diet coke once a day was too much to ask for out of life. I then walked outside and was warmly greeted by a group of the children who anxiously waited for us every morning to come out and play with them for a while before we started work. It then hit me like a ton of bricks. These children didn't own a pair of pants or even shoes and they were the happiest young people I had ever met. I woke up miserable because I couldn't have a diet coke. God has a way of answering prayers and my selfish one was answered loudly that morning in a lesson I will never forget. Who was I to complain about not having a diet coke while surrounded by children who had nothing and were always incredibly grateful for the little, they did have in life?

As the days turned into weeks, the children of Alpha quickly captured our hearts by their continuous smiles and laughing. Each Sunday after church their band and choir would perform a special concert for us and each evening after supper, we would have "World Cup" soccer matches between the U.S. and Jamaica. Happily, our U.S. team never could beat those kids from Jamaica.

I was fortunate that summer to spend a good bit of time with Newton, our chef, and over time came to know his life story and how he came to live at Alpha. His mother died while giving birth to him and his father, sadly, was a bad alcoholic. When he was about four years old, his dad went off on a drinking binge and left Newton in the shack on his own for days. When his dad finally returned, he realized that Newton had eaten all the food in their cupboard. He went into a drunken rage and decided he needed to punish Newton for not saving him some food. He took Newton outside and wrapped his two arms in towels and rags, dipped them into kerosene and lit Newton's arms on fire. Newton's right hand was completely burned off and his left hand had severe damage as well. He was moved to Alpha that afternoon.

When Newton arrived, he was obviously very traumatized. Sr. Susan, who ran the orphanage, took him under her wing. He quickly grew to love her like a mother and especially enjoyed when she would allow him to help her in the kitchen. As the years moved on, Sr. Susan realized that she needed to find a way to offer Culinary Arts as a trade option. It was the only profession that Newton had any interest in and one that he was passionate about pursuing. Sr. Susan arranged for a number of surgeries for Newton's arms through the great organization, Doctors without Borders. He became the first graduate of Alpha's culinary class and we were his first clients.

In the months that followed after we left, Newton began a catering business located at Don Bosco orphanage up in Mandeville, which was also operated by the Sisters. Over the years, his catering business has grown into one of the most successful on the island and all of the employees are graduates from the orphanages. In recent years, he has also opened a restaurant which likewise is successful and staffed by graduates of the Don Bisco orphanage.

I have worked with many young people in my life, but few faced as much trauma and difficulties in life as Newton. Yet, he remains one of the most positive and thankful people I have ever met. He has taught me much about forgiveness and letting go of one's hurts, and how it is more important to focus on those people in our life who have graced and helped us to succeed than hanging on to bitter memories of the past. Newton had every reason in life to be angry and resentful, yet he overcame his disabilities and became successful. He continues to be a model and inspiration to other young people who grow up in a similar fashion to what he knew. He will always be one of my heroes in life. As our time in Jamaica grew to a close, we knew that our lives were forever impacted by the joy and love shown to us by each of the children we had spent that summer with at Alpha.

Newton cooking one of his many great meals

Some of the Alpha Boys Band performing for us

"It is not the mountain we conquer, but ourselves."

– *Sir Edmund Hillary*

# 2

# Hiking the Blue Mountain

On the weekend before we came home from our Jamaican immersion experience, we got to live an adventure that remains one of the craziest experiences of our lives.

One of the staff members of Alpha advised us that before we left, we should take a hike up to the top of Jamaica's highest peak, the Blue Mountain. It would be a twenty-seven-mile trek with an elevation climb of over eight thousand feet. Br. Todd, our three college volunteers, Newton, Dunston, who was another of the recent Alpha graduates and I looked forward to the challenge and our two-day excursion.

One of the staff members dropped us off in the Alpha van at the base of the mountains at about 4:00 am and we began our long walk toward the top. The terrain was often rough and more difficult than we had imagined. By midday, we reached the level of the rainforest, which was a new and amazing experience for all of us. We walked through miles of fields with strange plants which we would later find out were ganja fields. We met some of the growers of these illegal drug fields who wanted to kill us for trespassing through their drug making industry, but thanks to Newton and Dunston speaking to them in a native patois, we were allowed to continue on our hike without being harmed.

We took our last rest break about two miles from the top. There was a little café there and we decided we would stop for breakfast on our return down the next morning. The final push to the top wasn't really hiking but rather bouldering and was slow going. We made it to the peak shortly before sunset and the views from the top were absolutely magnificent. We could see the entire way around the island and even the far-off coast of Cuba. Sunset was spectacular and we looked forward to enjoying a night of camping out in cooler weather than the small sauna like bedroom we had shared for the previous five weeks. We shared our supper supplies of peanut butter and jelly sandwiches and watched the red sky turn into a star lit night.

Our peaceful night quickly turned into a potential disaster when the winds picked up and the temperatures dropped to the low forties. If we did not find some form of shelter rapidly, some of our group would become very sick and some already began shivering from the fifty degree drop in temperature. We walked around the top of the Blue Mountain and were lucky to discover an abandoned building structure that had been made out of concrete. The roof was collapsing, the windows were all broken, but compared to the possibility of standing outside all night and freezing, it looked like a five-star hotel.

We were all overtired and soon spread out in this two-room structure to grab some needed and well-deserved sleep. I found some soft grass outside close to our hut and made a little bed for myself on the floor in the second room. I laid half of the sheet I had carried with me on top of the grass and the second half of the sheet over me. I used my backpack for a pillow and held the one small flashlight we had in my folded hands and started to drift off to sleep. After a while, I had a confusing sensation. I couldn't figure out how I could scratch my chin and still have my two hands gently folded with the flashlight in them. I turned on the flashlight and freaked out as I realized I wasn't scratching my chin, but instead that a giant rat was licking my face. I jumped to my feat which had the effect of sending the sheet on top of me into the air as well as the rat on top of the sheet into the collapsing roof overhead. The rest of our group quickly awoke to my screaming and asked what was wrong? All I kept screaming was "RATS, RATS, RATS." There must have been about twenty of them crawling around us at this point. We all rushed outside and soon realized that the rats were after our food bag and the smell of our peanut butter. Once we threw the contents of the bag away from the house, our nighttime visitors quickly left and pursued the peanut butter. Needless to say, everyone in our group, except me, thought that this was hilarious and the true highlight of the trip. I was freaked out and didn't sleep a wink that night. At one point I even saw one of our four legged little monsters walk past the door with a spoon in its mouth.

At about 4:00 am it became first light and white puffy clouds were passing through the two broken windows of our Holiday Inn. Jake, one of our college volunteers, awoke with a severe case of shin splints to the point he could barely walk. Jake was a big guy at about six foot six inches and two hundred and fifty pounds of pure muscle. He was a great rugby player in college and as strong as an ox. As we prepared to begin our descent down the mountain, one of the other guys offered to carry Jake's backpack to make it easier on him. I told Br. Todd to lead the hike down and that I would stay back with Jake and that we would meet at the café two miles below for breakfast. Within minutes the rest of our group were quickly out of sight as Jake slowly struggled one step at a time down across all the rocks and boulders. When we arrived at the café, we realized that the group had not waited there for us and had kept going. Unfortunately, we didn't have any of the money and could not get breakfast. We figured the group would wait for us before long and hopefully would have some supplies of fruit we had saved which we could eat. After a few hundred yards of slow hiking, Jake said he had to take a dump and asked me for the toilet paper. I told him that it was in Chris' backpack. He wasn't happy and for the next several miles he slowly walked, occasionally stopping to lean on his walking stick as he tried to push back the urge to go to the bathroom. This routine of walking a little and stopping continued until I heard him unleash a howling banshee type scream of "NOOOOO." He couldn't hold it in any longer and completely soiled himself. I had to walk about twenty yards ahead of him as the smell was sickening and he was getting angrier and more uncomfortable by the minute. It was bad enough that he could barely walk with his shin splints, but now he was walking as if he was riding a horse as he was carrying a full load.

Finally, we came around a bend in the trail to see the rest of our group lying in the grass waiting for us to catch up. I thought about warning them to leave their bags and run for their lives and not have to face Jake's fury, but they left us hanging at breakfast and frankly I wanted to see this unfold.

As Jake grew closer to them, they realized something was seriously wrong and soon the smell from Jake made the reality of the situation even more grim. They didn't know what to say, so Jake started explaining to them in very vivid terms with many adjectives just how angry he was at their insensitive behavior of not waiting for us at the designated breakfast spot. He proceeded to ask them if they had any "bleeping" idea what it was like to walk five 'bleeping" miles with "bleep" in their pants. Chris reached into his backpack and pulled out a roll of toilet paper, held it up and said, "Well, I guess you won't need this anymore?"

That was not the most intelligent choice of words that Chris might have used in this situation. Jake calmly walked over to him, grabbed him by the throat, left out another mighty scream, lifted him off the ground and then put him back on the ground and sat on his face.

A few miles further down the path we came to a stream in which Jake was able to wash himself but was in desperate need of baby powder as the rash had done considerable damage and would leave him very miserable and uncomfortable for many days to follow.

Further down the trail, we came across many local coffee farmers, who grow the world-famous Jamaican Blue Mountain coffee beans. One pound of this coffee can routinely be purchased in the U.S. for $49 per pound. We were able to purchase it directly from the local farmers for $1 per pound and bring many great presents of coffee back for our family members and friends. I have often wondered how many coffee vendors are making incredible profits and getting rich on this coffee at the expense of so many poor local coffee farmers who see none of those profits. Andrés Novela, a teacher and great Lay Marist at Monsignor Pace High School in Miami has been responding to this issue for many years in his own way. He went on a number of mission service trips to Honduras and met similar local coffee famers in that country. He has set up a way to help those local farmers and allow the teachers of his school to enjoy the best coffee break room of any school

I have ever visited. The school purchases all their coffee directly from those coffee farmers at fair market value. The farmers enjoy a just wage for their work and the teachers enjoy great and well-deserved coffee each day. Hopefully more conscious minded folks will look for creative ways to support Fair Trade products and not add to the exploitation of migrants and poor farmers in third world countries.

When we came to the end of our hike, we waited for the local bus to arrive and bring us back to the city of Kingston. The bus schedule indicated that the bus would operate every forty-five minutes. It eventually arrived after a four-hour wait in the hot sun. The bus itself was about the size of a shuttle bus used at airports in the USA to carry passengers to hotels or rental cars. There were about fifty people and two chickens already jammed into this small bus and I don't believe they were overly excited when we joined them, especially given the continued fragrance that came from Jake. We were delighted to finally make it back to Alpha and enjoy our last night there.

Looking back at that hike now and our time in Jamaica, I still hate rats and I wish Br. Todd and the group had waited at the designated breakfast point at the café as planned so Jake wouldn't have suffered what he endured. But I am nevertheless grateful for the entire experience. As difficult as those two days were for each of us both physically and in overcoming our fears of encountering drug gangs, rats, severe weather and Jake's unfortunate descent, we also came to appreciate that even in the worst of times, God was always present. He allowed us each to see his amazing beauty in our first experience of a rainforest, he gave us the opportunity to see an incredible sunset from the top of that mountain and most of all he allowed us to grow as a community of volunteers and appreciate each other in ways we never realized. God blessed our lives by allowing us the opportunity to come to know and love 185 of his most remarkable young people for the five weeks we spent with them at Alpha. Whatever little work we accomplished in our days at the orphanage was only a fraction of the impact that Newton and all those children permanently made on our lives. Br. Todd, Jake, Chris, Danny, Newton and I have often shared our memories of our days on the Blue Mountain and still smile and thank God for allowing us to have gone through it as it still offers us life lessons.

Our Jamaican Work Crew
Br. Leo Shea, Chris Kaiser, Br. Dan, Jake Morris
Br. Steve Synan, Danny Turner, Br. Todd

Hiking the Blue Mountain

"Twenty years from now you will be more disappointed by the things that you didn't do than by the ones you did do. So throw off the bowlines. Sail away from the safe harbor. Catch the trade winds in your sails. Explore. Dream. Discover."

*– Mark Twain*

# 3

## My '96 Campus Ministry Crew

In the late spring of 1995, I was asked to start Molloy's campus ministry program which for many years had been known at the school as the Religious Activities Office. It had not been utilized since Br. Mike Sheerin left the position a few years earlier. I reflected for some time on how I hoped to build up this important aspect of the school and the various retreat programs, liturgies, prayer services and possible service projects that might be part of it. The one aspect of the program that was very clear and important to me from the start was that I wanted it to be led by young people and to give the chosen campus ministry student team many opportunities to be a witness of faith and leadership to the wider school community. I also hoped that many of the events and programs that we would run through campus ministry would foster a deeper sense of what it means to be a Marist community and that it would promote ways to unite the faculty and students as a faith community centered on living and witnessing the gospel.

Through the grace of God, I was fortunate to select an amazing group of ten young men as Molloy's first campus ministry student leadership team. Dan Hurley, Jameson Mayr, Tony Mastropietro, Wolve Gardiner, Brian Hogan, Owen and Gary Corrigan, Joe Arevalo, John Gray and Joe Mannino became my "Campus Ministry Team." Little did I know at the time that they would accomplish so much, not only during that year as campus ministry leaders, but also in how they would continue to impact our wider world in the ways they chose to live their daily lives long after they graduated.

Prior to beginning our year working together, we spent a day together on retreat to plan out a roadmap for the various activities for the upcoming school year. One of the themes of that retreat was the concept that each of them needed to witness being servant leaders and to lead by example. Each of them committed to working together on all the larger events such as the coat drive, toy drive, numerous school liturgies, and the fast-a-thon. They would also individually commit to being a leader and weekly participant in one of the many service outreach programs that we sponsored.

Dan, Joe, John and Joe would be part of our student eucharistic ministers which consisted of about twenty-five seniors. These student eucharistic ministers not only distributed communion at school masses and retreats, but also brought the eucharist to patients at local hospitals and nursing homes on a weekly basis. This group of students had to complete training workshops sponsored by the diocese and were committed to meeting as a group bi-weekly to share about how their weekly eucharistic minister experience was going at the hospital or nursing home they were assigned. These opportunities for sharing were very moving at times. The student eucharistic ministers listened to each other share stories of the profound effect that this service experience of bringing Jesus to others would have on their lives. It seemed during every meeting, one or more of them would share how they were with a dying person or someone who was incredibly thankful to them for taking the time to pray and bring Jesus to that person. Many of the students who served as eucharistic ministers also became part of their parish team and many likewise would continue to be eucharistic ministers at the colleges they would eventually attend.

Jamison single handedly oversaw our largest service program which was a daily after school program at the Briarwood homeless shelter, located a few blocks from the school. He had been a volunteer in this program almost every day after school since his freshman year. The shelter housed ninety-one homeless families. Most were single moms with children. The shelter opened in 1992 and reached out to Molloy to see if the school would be interested in having some high school students involved in an afterschool tutoring program for the children who lived there. The shelter had a great staff and worked very hard to provide needed services for all its residents. It offered job training programs for the parents and helped find job placements as well. Once a family secured a job, the shelter worked to help assist the family in finding adequate and affordable housing. Most families remained at the shelter between six months to a year. The children were picked up by school bus and attended the local public school and were returned to the shelter each day at 3:00 pm. The parents were either working or attending a job training workshop until about 5:30 pm and so there was a daily void that needed to be filled in keeping the children of the shelter engaged until their parents were available. Br. Mike Sheerin and Mrs. Mary Ann Safrey initially oversaw the students from Molloy who would serve as tutors on a daily basis. After Br. Mike left, Mary Ann did everything she could do to keep it going with almost no support from the administration at that time.

By the time campus ministry took the program over in the fall of 1996, it needed a little revamping to get more Molloy student's engaged. Jameson and I made presentations in all the religion classes to recruit students to be needed tutors and we soon had enough Molloy students to ensure that twenty tutors worked at the shelter each day after school. This meant that twenty students committed to attending each Monday, twenty different students served as tutors on Tuesday, etc. Jamison coordinated the tutoring groups and would be at the shelter each day. I would stop each day around 5:00 pm after track practice and was always amazed to watch Jameson take control and see how much he enjoyed working with the homeless children. He would have the tutors help the children with their homework for the first ninety minutes and then organize various games for the remaining time. Jameson made our annual Molloy "Coats for Kids" drive and the toy drive extra special that year. He made a list of every child at the shelter which told us their jacket size and gender as well as any special instructions like a favorite sports team. Every child there was given a new coat as well as a hat and gloves. Jackets were also provided for all the parents of the children. Jamison coordinated a Santa letter writing campaign among the children of the shelter and with the help of Molloy's toy drive, Santa was able to provide every child with their requested gifts that Christmas. Jamison even got to be one of Santa's special helpers at the Christmas party that our campus ministry team sponsored. By the end of the school year, Jamison received national recognition for his outstanding commitment to helping to improve the quality of life among the homeless community of the Briarwood shelter during his four years of high school. Jameson's passion for helping the least favored didn't end in high school. During his college years, he became an active leader in the Special Olympics program, which he continues to do today with the assistance of his own children. Jameson also volunteered on numerous occasions during my years of working in Appalachia and remains a most generous supporter to any Marist service project.

The Corrigan twins, Wolve, Brian and Tony played a unique role as part of our campus ministry team that year. They were part of the track team, which I also coached. It was a special year for that track team as they brought much success and glory to the school by winning both the indoor and outdoor city championships, as well as successfully competing at the prestigious Millrose Games, the Penn Relays and the Colonial Relays. Because we had track practice every day, they were not required to participate in one of the normal campus ministry weekly service activities such as being a eucharistic minister or working at the shelter, but instead would commit to working with me on numerous days a week after our track practices ended and often on Saturdays after our track meets. They would help me do all the unheralded types of jobs such as setting up the gymnasium for school liturgies, preparing materials for upcoming Esopus retreats and Encounters, helping to organize the thousands of coats and toys that would be donated to our annual drives and to help deliver them all. Between the coat drive and toy drive, there were over thirty van loads of deliveries made that year. We spent a great amount of time in the school's old silver bullet van and ate a lot of pizza on long nights of work.

I remain deeply proud of all that the '96 Molloy campus ministry team accomplished during that inaugural year, but even more fulfilled knowing how each of them continue to be faith-filled and incredible men who every day live Molloy's school motto, "Not for School, but for Life."

Jamison watching the children at the Briarwood Shelter during a break from homework

Enjoying time with the CM crew in Esopus

"The young do not know enough to be prudent, and therefore they attempt the impossible, and achieve it, generation after generation. "

*– Pearl S. Buck*

# 4

## Where two or three are gathered

In the summer of '96, I was talking with Br. Steve Urban, an older but very active brother at the school, about ways to further expand campus ministry in the upcoming school year. He attended all our student retreats and was a great witness of faith and fidelity to the entire school community. He suggested that we should start a weekly prayer group after school. We decided we would call it, "The Lantern" which has a very special meaning in our Marist history.

In February of 1826. St Marcellin and another brother by the name of Br. Stanaslas had hiked several miles across the mountains near La Valla in France to see a sick brother in one of our other communities. On their return journey, they were caught in a terrible snowstorm with blizzard-like conditions. They became lost and their situation became incredibly dangerous. St. Marcellin instructed Br. Stanislas to join him in reciting a special prayer to Mary, the mother of God, so that she might intercede on their behalf and save them from pending doom. As soon as they finished saying this prayer, called the Memorae, they saw the light of a lantern coming from the top of a nearby hill. They followed the light and were led to the farmhouse of a family by the name of Donnet. Their lives were saved as they stayed with this family until it was safe for them to continue their journey. What makes the story even more interesting is the fact that Mr. Donnet had gotten dressed and went outside to go to the barn area to check his cattle. This was something he normally would never do as he had built a special enclosed passageway between his house and the barn so he wouldn't have to face bad weather when checking on the animals. We as Marists believe it was the intercession of our Good Mother that prompted Mr. Donnet to go out into the snow with his lantern that night and help save Champagnat and Stanaslas and thus the significance of the lantern in our Marist history.

When school began in September, Br. Steve and I advertised through daily school announcements as well as posters around the school of the first meeting of Molloy's new prayer group, "The Lantern." We were hopeful that it would be a success. When the day arrived and we went to the school chapel for the prayer group, we found only two freshman students there, namely Bobby Delay and Joe Forgione. Although I was a little disappointed in the poor showing of students, we continued on with the prayer we had planned. When we ended the prayer, these two students seemed excited and said that our praying with them showed them that we as Brothers really did believe and live the gospel passage that says, "Where two or three are gathered, I too am there." Their words of encouragement meant a great deal to both Br. Steve and me. We all agreed that we would meet again the following week, but that we would each ask one other person to join us. Our prayer group grew to ten students and a few Brothers on week two and within about a month we had a consistent group of almost sixty students, faculty members and Brothers who joined together weekly in prayer. By Thanksgiving, I asked our two original student members and a few other regular attendees if they would be interested in taking turns planning and leading the prayer in the weeks and months that followed. Even after twenty-four years, "The Lantern" prayer group at Molloy still continues to meet weekly and is still led by student leaders. Hundreds of young people and faculty members have been part of this prayer group over the years and it would not have happened without the willingness of those two young freshmen to say yes that first day as well as want to continue coming back. In the years I was at Molloy and attended the prayer group I was always struck by the depth and sincerity of so many young people to openly live and witness their faith.

Both Bobby and Joe would become great campus ministry leaders at Molloy. They helped thousands of our homeless brothers and sisters by their dedication to assisting in our outreach programs like the coat drive, toy drive, Briarwood shelter programs as well as on mission service trips to work at homeless centers in Wheeling, WV and Lawrence, MA. They shared their faith with younger students as leaders on school retreats in Esopus; they spent weeks of their summer volunteering as counselors at our special needs' camps in Esopus but most of all they witnessed to everyone who knew them that young people can make a difference and need not be afraid to live the gospel.

After I left Molloy in '98, I moved to West Virginia to begin working at Bishop Donahue High School. On one occasion while Bobby was in college, he called me and asked if I needed any help as he was willing to fly down during his college spring break if he was needed. We always needed assistance. He was to arrive on a Sunday afternoon at Pittsburgh airport. As it turned out, I actually drove my car to the airport on that Friday to fly to NY so that I could drive back a rental truck with donated lockers for a locker room we were building at the school. My plan was to drive the truck down on Sunday and stop at the airport to meet Bobby; give him my car keys so he could follow me back to West Virginia in my car and enjoy catching up with him during the week that would follow. My drive down that Sunday was certainly an adventure as I had to drive through a late spring snowstorm. When I finally arrived at the airport to meet Bobby, I realized that the truck was too big to fit inside the parking garage. I drove up to the arrivals pick up area which seemed deserted and parked there. I wondered if flights had been canceled due to the storm. No one was in sight, so I decided to take a quick run into the terminal to look at the airline monitors to see if Bobby's flight had in fact landed. Before I could make it to the door, two police cars came screeching into the arrivals area. The officers got out of their cars, drew their weapons and started screaming at me, "You in the blue jacket hands in the air." I quickly complied and they asked me what was in the truck. They didn't seem to believe my story that I was transporting lockers and picking up a college student. They began to tell me that it was illegal to bring a rental truck within a certain distance of the airport and wanted to know if I had ever heard of the Oklahoma bombing. Luckily for me, Bobby walked out of the terminal at this point and the officers allowed us to leave.

Even after all these years, Joe and Bobby still keep in touch with me and continue to be men of faith, integrity and never afraid to help someone in need. Whenever I return to visit Molloy and pass the school chapel, I think of them and the legacy of the school's Lantern prayer group that would not exist without them. Young people still gather in that chapel weekly to pray because of the impact these two young freshmen had at Molloy. Every year thousands of new freshman students enter our schools and I can only imagine the potential for greatness that lies in the hearts and minds of each one of them and pray that God allows them the opportunities to become an impact on the lives of others.

Some of the original Lantern Prayer Group.
Joe and Bobby are the sutdents on the far left.

"Young people need models, not critics."

– *John Wooden*

# 5

## The little engine that could.

When I began working at Bishop Donahue, one of the first things I did was start a cross-country team at the school. Unlike my days at Molloy where almost one hundred freshmen would join cross-country every year, I had a team of three runners. Brian "Blinky" McCann was my sole senior runner. He also played on the school's football team. We had to be creative to get him his needed weekly mileage and not miss football practice. He would play games on Friday nights and then run cross-country races early on Saturday mornings. He quickly developed into a solid distance runner and became the school's first athlete to qualify for the WV state xc championships at which he medaled. As our team was very small, I had plenty of time to get to know and work with our school's runners. Bryan and two fellow senior classmates also became the leaders of the campus ministry program I was beginning at the school. He was a born leader and as the year progressed, I grew to respect Bryan even more as I came to know his story. He was an only child and raised by a divorced mom. His dad was not part of his life and most of his family were pushing him to go work in the local coal industry. He was bright, motivated, hardworking and wanted something more out of life. After attending a Marist Encounter retreat in Esopus, he was really on fire and wanted to become more active in living his faith. He helped run all the underclass retreats and quickly became an inspiring young man willing to be a needed role model and example of someone who was not afraid to live and share his faith. During the spring track season, Bryan continued to excel as a runner and qualified for the state track championships in multiple events. He medaled in the 3200-meter race and began a streak of Bishop Donahue athletes being very competitive at the state meet for years to come. After graduation, Bryan attended Duquesne University where he not only ran but would eventually earn a law degree. He continued to stay involved as a leader during his college years with both retreats at Bishop Donahue as well as at our Marist Encounter retreats in Esopus. Today he serves our country in the FBI.

During my six years at Bishop Donahue our little track team went from my driving the entire team to track meets in my car to our needing a large school bus as the number of participating athletes grew each year. "Our little engine that could" became a real family and success story as the kids worked hard daily. Our volunteer coaching staff were remarkable and donated endless hours to help allow each athlete to become the best they could be. Joe Polus, Fred Treedlie, Marty Wingert, Eddie Blankenship, and Fr. Terry Adams would be the driving force behind the numerous team championships our athletes would win and often against schools much bigger in size than the total of eight-five in our entire student body at the time. The parents of our track team likewise provided tremendous support in helping with numerous fundraisers to help allow our athletes the opportunity to travel down state for the state championships as well as purchase needed equipment, uniforms as well as enjoy many great meals after track meets. The track coaches at Archbishop Molloy also greatly helped make the success of those Bishop Donahue teams a reality. Not only did they generously donate used equipment such as hurdles, shot puts, relay batons, and stop watches, but also were willing to offer coaching clinics to some of our better athletes in pre-season to help them prepare for their events. During one of those weekend clinics the Bishop Donahue athletes got to work out with Kawan Lovelace, a Molloy alumnus and a track Olympian. Experiences like that allowed those athletes to believe that dreams are possible and hard work can make them become realities.

One of the many highlights of my experience working with that team was the story of Matt Beiter. He joined our team as a sophomore and was a good athlete who was willing to try multiple events such as long jump, high jump and hurdles. He seemed to have natural talent as a high jumper and did well during his first season. During his junior year I brought him and a few of our other promising athletes up to New York to work out with some of the coaches at Molloy, who had great experience in coaching all the specialized events such as jumping, hurdles, pole vault, etc. Matt learned some great drills and was willing to work hard and do whatever it took to improve. We didn't always have much needed track equipment, so we had to be creative to find ways for him to practice. Our first high jump pit consisted of bales of straw with an old mattress on top covered by a blue tarp. Matt's perseverance, talent and hard work paid off as he enjoyed a senior season for the ages. He would be the Mason-Dixon conference, OVAC conference, West Virginia Region I and State Champion in the high jump. He set meet records that still stand in almost all those championships. He also qualified and competed in the Penn Relays, Golden South and the National USA Track and Field Youth Championships. He became West Virginia's first and only national champion in his last meet as a high school student. He earned a track scholarship to Wheeling Jesuit University and went on to proudly serve our country in the armed forces. Today, he is a devoted husband, loving father and as humble and unassuming as the first day I met him.

Matt's story of becoming a national champion illustrates that we should never underestimate the potential of any young person but rather find ways and opportunities to allow those young people a chance to dream and make it a reality.

Matt Beiter, 2004 USA Track & Field National Youth Champion

One of the many BDHS championship relay teams
Celebrating their victory at their Prom
Well done Rusty, Jody, Ed and Shawn

"Young people should be at the forefront of global change and innovation. Empowered, they can be key agents for development and peace. If, however, they are left on society's margins, all of us will be impoverished. Let us ensure that all young people have every opportunity to participate fully in the lives of their societies."

– *Kofi Annan*

# 6

## Miracles in the Mountain State

My six years serving at Bishop Donahue High School in McMechen, WV were certainly my most enjoyable and rewarding years in ministry. That little school was an incredible faith community and became a school that embraced the Marist charism in real and powerful ways.

During my last three years there, I had the grace to come to know four amazing young girls that will always remain as true heroes in my life. Jobeth Gross, Danielle Block, Melissa McCulley and Katie Beiter entered Bishop Donahue as freshmen in the fall of 2001. They came from four different grade schools but quickly became close friends and they seemed inseparable. They each played together on the school's volleyball, basketball, softball and track teams. Within weeks they became actively involved in our school's campus ministry programs and a part of our Marist Youth Group. They sang in the choir and performed each year as a quartet in the school's annual musical. I nicknamed them "The Four Musketeers."

Over the years I worked with them they grew into great retreat leaders and were always willing to show up to help with any project, especially if it involved helping those in need. Rose Hart, a local friend of mine, started a great organization called, Appalachian Outreach, whose mission was to assist our many struggling brothers and sisters in the southern part of the state. She would send truckloads of needed supplies down to the southern counties and often needed help with the loading of those trucks. The Musketeers were regular truck loaders in those years. Rose shared with us on one of our first days of working with her that she was trying to gather supplies to make simple Christmas gifts for those people she served that lacked the most basic of necessities. The girls came up with the idea of "Shoebox Santas." They spent days travelling to every shoe store in the Ohio Valley asking for donations of empty shoe boxes and then helped create a campaign leading up to Christmas to gather items to put in the boxes such as toiletries, sox, gloves, hats, children's books, etc. After all the donations of items were collected, they assembled the boxes and then wrapped them as Christmas presents. In that first year, more than two hundred and fifty "Shoebox Santas" were delivered downstate personally by the Four Musketeers. By the time they were seniors, the "Shoebox Santas" program had expanded and was adopted by many other local churches and schools to help bring the annual donations of "Shoebox Santas" to over five thousand each year. The Musketeers' simple idea of finding a way to help others less fortunate continues to be implemented by Appalachian Outreach each Christmas.

Each of those springs, I ran a mission service trip down to these areas in southern West Virginia to help restore a number of homes that had been badly damaged from recent floods. The Four Musketeers always made those weeks not only meaningful in regard to the works we accomplished, but also experiences of great joy from their constant laughter.

Each of the girls had unique and special stories. Jobeth lost her mom to cancer a few years before high school and Bob, her dad, was on disability from a work accident. During her sophomore year, their home was destroyed by a devastating flood and she lost most of her personal items. She stayed at the homes of the other Musketeers until her dad could secure a new place for them to live. Also, during her sophomore year, she lost her only remaining aunt, who was tragically shot at a mall in Ohio by someone in a passing car. This was her favorite aunt, the sister of her mom, and the one who would bring her shopping for homecoming dresses. I have met very few young people that had to face as much tragedy and loss in their lives as Jobeth did in her first sixteen years. What remains most remarkable to me is that she refused to allow those tragic events in her life to stop her from achieving her goals and dreams. She would rather dedicate her hard work to her mom and know that both her mom and aunt were smiling down on her and proud of who she was becoming in life. When younger students would complain about trivial things in their lives, she would quickly share some of her story and help that younger student to appreciate what they had instead of complaining about it.

Melissa lost her dad at the age of ten and was raised by a most loving and incredible mother. She has two older siblings who both attended Bishop Donahue as well. Danielle had an older sister and two amazing parents, who were very involved in her life. Katie was the third of six children that would each attend Bishop Donahue. Her parents were incredible people of faith and like the parents of the other Musketeers would unselfishly volunteer at Bishop Donahue for almost all events.

I left Bishop Donahue to move to New Jersey at the end of their junior year but promised to return to be present at some of the major events of their senior year such as Homecoming, Prom, and the musical. I met them in Esopus when they made their Marist Encounter retreat and they traveled up to New Jersey for their Thanksgiving break with Danielle's parents and Melissa's mom. We toured New York and had a great time together. Melissa and I share the same birthday in mid-May, and they decided they would come back up to New Jersey to celebrate with me. Katie could not travel as she had qualified in hurdles for the state track meet. Jodi and Courtney Block and Roxzane again escorted the remaining Musketeers up for that weekend. Because they had already seen NYC on their previous trip, I wanted to do something special for their graduations that they might enjoy while in the New York area. I booked the three of them on a small sightseeing plane that would fly out of Linden airport in New Jersey and allow them to see the sights of NYC from the air. We all drove down to the airport on Saturday May 21ST and the three girls took off. The plane arrived back shortly after takeoff as Melissa felt sick. The pilot said he could still take someone else for the ride if we wanted and so Danielle's dad, Courtney, gladly joined them for the excursion. It would be the last time we ever saw them as the plane tragically crashed onto Coney Island and killed them all.

It remains the worst day in my life and one that none of us will ever fully recover. The days that followed were filled with great sorrow, many tears and two of the largest attended funerals ever in the state of West Virginia as we said goodbye to our "Three Angels." Some nice memorials would eventually be held in their honor. The street in front of Bishop Donahue was renamed "Three Angels Way." A scholarship fund was established in their honor at the school and many "Three Angels" blood drives were held. Danielle and Jobeth were also posthumously elected into the Bishop Donahue Hall of Fame.

Melissa and Katie lost their best friends and would endure many tough days as a result of that disaster, but both managed to graduate from Wheeling Jesuit University. Katie is now happily married with her own children and is working as a nurse. Melissa still works close to home and remains committed to helping others. She always takes time off from work anytime I bring a group of young people down to West Virginia on a mission service trip and helps coordinate many of the details as well as share in our nightly prayer reflections.

A day never passes when I don't think about our "Three Angels." Every day I pray that God will continue to give Jodi Block and Bob Gross the strength they need to carry on. I know our "Three Angels" in heaven are watching over them and all of us.

The "Four Musketeers" will always remain heroes in my life and a reminder of the pure joy and goodness that can be found in all young people. Even though two of them were taken from us far too young, their legacy remains alive in the hearts of all of us that were blessed to know them as well as each Christmas when the miracle of "Shoebox Santas" are delivered.

The Four Musketeers

"Everyone can be great because everyone can serve."

– *Martin Luther King, Jr.*

# 7

## Many hands make light work

After moving from West Virginia, I spent the next seven years working at Roselle Catholic High School. I enjoyed serving in many roles at the school during those years, but my most memorable days often involved helping with the school's vibrant and active Marist Youth program. We hosted many events and opportunities for the RC community to join together for prayer and in many service activities. Our future student leaders of the Marist Youth group would attend, either in their sophomore or junior year, a large Marist Youth gathering held each May. Marist Youth from all our schools around the country as well as Marist Youth from Canada and Mexico would participate in this annual gathering. Students would then return to the schools and be the leaders of the local Marist Youth groups at their respective schools for their remaining high school years. Our leaders worked hard to ensure that the RC Marist Youth group would become the standard for what a youth group could accomplish.

Each spring we traveled to West Virginia to connect with my many friends there and assist local families in that area that were in great need. All of the expenses of the trip were raised throughout the year by the Marist Youth group in a number of creative ways. We hosted the Champagnat Games each November which was a series of basketball, volleyball and hockey games between the RC faculty and students. The event would draw a large crowd of students and parents who would watch many of the older faculty take one for the team. At Christmas time, groups of students would sign up to build gingerbread houses which they had to get a sponsor to buy. All money raised from the sale of the gingerbread houses directly helped us repair real houses for those less fortunate. I was always impressed that so many young people were willing to not only help raise the money for this trip but were so excited to give up their spring break to help others rather than enjoy Disney or other vacation spots like many of their friends. We actually had to hold a lottery for each of these trips as the demand from students who wanted to participate was more than we could ever bring.

John Allen, a graduate of RC and a general contractor, would take his vacation every year to join our annual service trip. His participation allowed our young people the opportunity to work on some very significant building projects that could never have been attempted without John's expertise, guidance and tools. Over the years we roofed homes, built handicap bathrooms, handicap ramps, decks and other major construction projects for some very grateful recipients. Each night we shared in a prayer and reflection on the workday and how the person encountered God that day. During one of those reflections a student, named Kristina spoke about how she wished more young people from RC could get to experience all the opportunities to serve that she had during the trip. As the conversation moved along, it was pointed out that we certainly didn't need to drive ten hours in a school bus to find people with needs. The reality was we could travel less than ten minutes from the school to find similar situations of poverty and need. The fruits of that continued conversation turned into the Roselle Catholic summer days of service.

Following that trip, each June when school ended, the RC community was invited to spend the first week of their summer vacation in the service of others. More than one hundred and twenty-five students, faculty and parents would engage in this incredible week of allowing young people to help make a real difference in the lives of many people and families. Everyone arrived each morning at school by 8:00 am. Br. Raoul, teachers and parent volunteers had arrived by 6:00 am to prepare breakfast for everyone. After breakfast, we gathered for a morning prayer and broke the students and adults into their assigned work groups that were led by our Marist Youth Leaders. Many teachers volunteered their time to drive all the school buses which were needed to transport folks to the various work sites each day. Projects included working at a local food bank, Habitat for Humanity, volunteering to do needed painting jobs for nearby parishes, schools or elderly folks, garbage clean-ups at local beaches and county parks, as well as many needed projects at Roselle Catholic itself. Students returned to RC for lunch which again was prepared by our volunteer cooks. The groups were mixed up in the afternoon and students went off for their second work session of the day. When they returned from work, they enjoyed a great dinner, and everyone gathered for an evening prayer and reflection. On the last night, we had a big cookout followed by games and water balloon activities.

One of the more significant projects that was accomplished through the RC summer service days was the creation and building of the RC Labyrinth. The concept of a labyrinth goes back to ancient times. Many religions and cultures have the practice of going on a pilgrimage. Muslims will often travel to Mecca on pilgrimage, Catholics to the Holy Land or Marial shrines, such as Lourdes, and many in the Jewish faith to the wailing wall. In medieval times, when wars prevented folks from making a pilgrimage, utilizing a prayer labyrinth became popular. Numerous designs were created but always had one path leading to the center and the same path leading back out. The idea was to slowly walk toward the center while reflecting on your inward journey, spend some time at the center of the Labyrinth speaking to God and then allow God to walk with you as you return back into the world. This meditative walk was a simple and symbolic way of making a personal pilgrimage. One of the more famous Labyrinths in the world is the one in the Cathedral of Chartres, near Paris. This was the design we chose for the RC labyrinth.

K.C. Murray, one of our senior Marist Youth leaders spearheaded the project with Ed Kennedy, who was an RC parent and landscaper by trade. The idea was to place the labyrinth on the grass in the main quadrangle of the school so that this prayer space would become the centerpiece of the school. As the school would soon be celebrating its 50th anniversary, having students build the labyrinth seemed like a great gift from the students to the school community in honor of this special upcoming occasion. K.C. carefully painted the design onto the grass in the quadrangle; it was sixty feet in diameter. He and Ed then carefully dug all the sod out between the lines of the painted design. The work groups assigned to work on the labyrinth during the summer service days helped level the entire path, put down sand and then lay eight thousand brinks which would become the walkway. John Allen assisted with the cutting of brinks for the curved edges. On the last evening of the 2008 RC summer service days more than one hundred and fifty students, faculty and parent volunteers gathered for the first prayer around the school's new prayer space. It remains a testament to what young people can accomplish in only a few days and a space that is still frequently utilized by many for prayer and personal reflection.

The Roselle Catholic
Labyrinth
Built during 2008 RC
Summer Service Days

First day of 2008 RC
Summer Service Days
Prayer around the
painted Labyrinth.
By Friday it was
completed.

The Celebration of the
RC 50th Anniversary

"The young generation can influence their elders and can make them understand the environmental problems that are faced by us today. The youth can make them see that our environment is deteriorating day by day."

– *Chief Oren Lyons*

# 8

# Our Homeless Brothers and Sisters

One of the greatest religion teachers I ever had a chance to work with was Mary Byrne Hoffmann who taught at Roselle Catholic. She was incredibly creative and stirred a deep passion and hunger for spirituality among many of her students. One of the great gifts she brought to the Roselle Catholic community was the introduction of the Bridges Outreach Program. Bridges Outreach Inc. is a non-profit organization whose sole mission is to assist the many needs of the large homeless population living in the NYC area. Bridges Outreach partners with numerous churches and schools to assist them in providing needed food and clothing to our many homeless brothers and sisters living on the streets. A parish or school who establishes a Bridges program commits to organizing the collection of needed clothing and providing food for about one hundred homeless persons and delivering those items personally on a designated date to the homeless at two or three drop off points. The organization took the name Bridges because many of the homeless in NYC lived under actual bridges.

The Roselle Catholic Bridges program committed to doing five Bridges trips a year, usually in the winter months. A few days before a designated trip, students would organize the clothing that had been collected and get it sorted by blankets, coats, sweaters, underwear, sox, etc. and by size and gender. On the day of a trip, another group of students volunteered to make the needed bags of food to be distributed. These bags included fresh sandwiches made by the students, a snack, a piece of fruit and a juice drink. Students normally prepared between two hundred to three hundred such bags of food.

Like most of the service opportunities at Roselle Catholic, a lottery system was needed to select students for a particular Bridges trip as there were always more students who wanted to assist than could be accommodated on the trip. The group of students and faculty members actually going on the Bridges trip would meet at about 6:00 pm. They would load one or two school buses with all the items to be given out and then meet in the chapel to pray prior to departing at 7:00 pm. Senior students who had been on previous trips would lead the prayer and remind first timers that the purpose of the trip is not to "fix" or "save" the homeless. Rather it was about accepting them as fellow brothers and sisters and building relationships with them. Those prayer leaders shared that those going on the trip would receive equally as much from our homeless friends as anything we might offer them. Prayer always concluded with the recitation of the St. Francis prayer, "Make me a channel of your peace."

During one of our winter trips, we were joined by two special guests; two Marist Brothers, who were part of our General Council in Rome and were making their official visit to the USA Province. These types of visits occurred every three to four years. The Superior General of the Marist Brothers and the members of the General Council oversaw the entire Marist World which is located in eighty-two countries around the globe. When such visits occur in a province, the General counselors meet with the leadership team of a province, visit some of the communities, meet the young brothers in formation and try to attend at least one event with young people. The General Couselors who were visiting on this particular night had requested attending a Bridges trip as they had heard about the program being a very successful form of outreach to the homeless of NYC. The two visiting Brothers fully engaged in the trip and helped make sandwiches and pack the bus prior to leaving for NYC. As it turned out, this trip occurred on one of the coldest nights in the history of NYC with a wind chill factor at minus twenty-five degrees.

When we arrived in NYC and made our two designated stops, we met many of the "regulars" who were usually there whenever we made a trip. Those friendly faces were always glad to see us and beyond grateful for whatever help we could provide on a given night. So often, if we had extra bags of food and offered them to a homeless person, the response would be, "I have enough, give it to that person over there, he needs it more than me." Sadly, on this given night there were more than twenty young children waiting at our stops. We were grateful to be able to distribute hats and gloves to them as most did not have a set and were visibly freezing in the frigid night air. When we were finishing up at our second stop, one homeless gentleman arrived a little late and enquired if there were any medium sized jackets left. He was not wearing one. Unfortunately, by this stage of the trip, we had given away all the jackets we had collected. Tyler, one of our students, told the man to hang on as he thought that there may be one more jacket on the bus. The student went back onto the bus and quickly returned with a medium sized leather jacket. Our homeless friend had tears of gratitude in his eyes when the student presented him with the jacket.

On the morning after the trip, we met the students who attended the trip in the student chapel for prayer and an opportunity for them to share about their experience. Our two General Councilors joined us for this prayer and sharing. The students were happy and grateful they were able to help so many on such a terribly cold night. Many spoke of their gratitude for all they had in their own lives, especially after witnessing all the homeless children on the previous night. One of the visiting Brothers then shared that he did not sleep at all after the trip as he felt completely ashamed. He explained that when he found out he would be going on this trip to meet actual homeless people in NYC, he decided to leave his wallet, his watch and all his valuables locked up in his room at the Brothers residence for fear that he might be robbed by one of the homeless. He also explained that he had been sitting on the bus directly behind Tyler on the way into NYC. He saw Tyler take off his leather jacket before the second stop and leave it on his seat as they began to unload all the stuff from the bus. He shared that he had never been so humbled when he reflected on how a young person could so easily give away his most valuable possession to a homeless person and he himself had been so fearful of what a homeless person might steal from him. Young people can often be our greatest teachers.

One of the many RC Bridges Trips.
Pictured under the Brooklyn Bridge.
One of our regular drop off points.

"Don't worry when you are not recognized, but strive to be worthy of recognition."

*– Abraham Lincoln*

# 9

## The Power of One

In the summer of 2008, I travelled to Sydney, Australia for two weeks with members of the RC Marist Youth group to attend the inaugural Marist Youth International Festival and the World Youth Days. Each program was one week-long. The Marist Festival welcomed more than four hundred and fifty young Marists from every corner of the planet and was a magnificent celebration of our common charism. The days of the festival consisted of powerful keynote talks, workshops, daily opportunities for prayers and a chance to meet fellow Marists from across the globe and realize that we all shared a similar vision and had many of the same values.

The highlight of the trip for me was during the opening ceremony when two Marist symbols were carried in during a procession. One was of a lantern and the second was a large heart that would be placed near a statue of our Good Mother. It was a replica statue of the one that St. Marcellin had prayed with during his own lifetime. He also had a similar but much smaller heart locket and placed it around the neck of his statue of our Good Mother. Each day he would put the names of brothers that needed prayers into that locket. Champagnat symbolically wanted to entrust whatever intentions he had on any given day directly into the heart of Mary. The names of all participants at the festival were placed into this symbolic heart being presented at the opening ceremony. What made this event so powerful for me was the fact that a young student, named Sammy, would be the one to carry in the heart.

Sammy was one of ten students attending the Marist Festival from our LaValla school in Cambodia. The LaValla school was started almost thirty years ago by a Marist Brother who realized that children born in Cambodia with any physical or mental abnormalities would be thrown to the gutter. Every child at this orphanage school is handicapped in some way and was abandoned by their families. Sammy was born with no functioning arms or legs and spent his entire life in a wheelchair. When I reflect on our Marist Mission, which is to make Jesus known and loved, especially among the least favored, it would be hard to imagine any better representation than Sammy to be the one to literally carry in our symbolic Marist heart. For a young person that will never walk, his actions and witness were more powerful than anyone else at the festival. I was graced by the opportunity to get to know him a little that week and the impression he made on me will forever be in my heart.

During our second week in Sydney, we attended the World Youth Days, which were started by Pope John Paul II and happen every few years in a different country. I have been fortunate to have been able to attend the event several times with young people in Denver, Toronto, Sydney and Rio de Janeiro. The best part of WYD is seeing up to a million young people from all over the world be completely on fire about living and sharing their faith. So many young people who have attended these events have made serious commitments to live their faith in a deeper and more profound way. Many vocations to religious life and the priesthood came from young people who attended these events, while many others dedicated themselves to deepen their prayer lives and find concrete opportunities to better live the gospel in a more genuine way.

As a result of our experience at that Marist Festival, many of our USA Marist schools now utilize a similar prayer service entrusting the names of all faculty members, students and parents to Mary in a heart locket in their respective school chapels. While I have not yet had the privilege to visit or work at our LaValla school in Cambodia, I have been lucky enough to know and hear many stories from several Brothers and Lay Marists who have had that opportunity. I am grateful that in the USA, we at least are responding to children with similar difficult disabilities through our special needs camps each summer in Esopus.

The Marist International Festival 2008
Some of our RC group with Sammy

Taize Prayer at the Marist International Festival. The
symbolic Marist heart was featured at all our prayers.
Sammy had carried it into the opening ceremony.

"Try not to become a man of success but rather try to become a man of value."

– *Albert Einstein*

# 10

# A Girl with a Big Heart and a Big Hammer

Ellen Salmi started as a freshman at Roselle Catholic the same year I moved there from West Virginia. She would become one of the most inspiring young people I would ever have the privilege to work with and someone who continues to amaze me by the many ways she continues to impact her world.

I first got to know her as part of the Roselle Catholic track team as I coached her in high jump. She also quickly became involved in the school's "Bridges Program," which I wrote about in an earlier chapter. After one of our trips to bring needed clothing and food to our friends on the streets in NYC, she asked if she could have some space in the large three car garage that is under the Brothers' house on the property of the school. She raised some money through writing letters to family and friends and earned enough to build a large storage area complete with sufficient shelves to hold more than one hundred large plastic containers. Her storage space became the "RC Bridges Closet" and is carefully organized into sections for all types of clothing, jackets, underwear, hats, and gloves for boys, girls, men and women and for all sizes. There is also a section for children's books, toiletries and needed supplies for each trip such as sandwich bags, etc. The closet is still being utilized today.

As she continued at Roselle Catholic, she evolved into one of the leaders of our Marist Youth group and helped make many great projects a reality. Like other impressive young people, I was graced to know, she was a person who was always willing to help even for the worst and most boring jobs such as folding and putting eight thousand letters into envelopes a few times a year. On one of our spring break service trips to West Virginia, she worked at replacing a roof for a handicapped person with John Allen. They worked through horribly cold weather and even in the snow. At the end of the week, John rewarded her with the hammer she used all week to drive in the nails of that roof. That same hammer is still being put to good use by Ellen.

After high school, she continued to stay involved in Marist projects through her commitment as a leader in the Marist Young Adult Program. She led retreats and Marist Youth gatherings, attended a pilgrimage to l'Hermitage and joined numerous other prayer and Marist service activities.

After graduating from Villanova, she followed her call to live the Marist charism in a deeper way by becoming a two-year volunteer with the Marist Missionary Sisters in Senegal, Africa. While on assignment there, she came to discover that most of the children of her village did not know how to read because they had no access to books. She wrote for grants, secured the funding and literally built a children's library for the village, using the same hammer given to her by John Allen. I went to visit her during her time in Senegal and it was amazing to see the love and appreciation the children of that village had for her. Most people would not accomplish in their lifetimes as much, in terms of dramatically impacting the lives of the poorest of our world, as she had done by the age of twenty-three.

Her journey of faith continued after she returned from Africa. She completed her master's degree at Catholic Theological Union in Chicago where she met her future husband, Josh. After they finished their studies, they were hired by the Diocese of Lexington, KY to become the first lay administrators and Parish Life Directors of Holy Cross Parish in Jackson, KY. The parish is in the poorest county in the state. Apart from running the parish, she and Josh also purchased and moved onto a beautiful fifty-acre farm. Their vision is to turn it into a Catholic Worker Farm to serve many purposes. With the help of John Allen and one of our Marist service trips, they were able to convert an old barn on the property into a place that can now host meals for the local community. In addition, they are planning the renovation of the upstairs area of the barn to become a temporary shelter for women and children. There is no such facility in their entire county.

They plan to eventually host volunteers to live and work on the property and help them with the development of an organic farm. They hope to also host retreatants who may wish to enjoy the many trails on the property and stay in one of the hermitages they are in the process of building.

Over the past sixteen years, I have admired and watched Ellen share her capacity to love others and be an incredible and genuine witness of the Gospel in all aspects of her life. She never ceases to astound me, and her inspiration always challenges me to want to live my own faith more authentically each day. Today she also serves as a member of the inaugural USA Council of Lay Marist and is the chairperson of their Marist Formation committee.

One of the handicap ramps,
Ellen and our RC Marist Youth built in West Virginia

Ellen Salmi with young people in Senegal

"How wonderful it is that nobody need wait a single moment before starting to improve the world."

– Anne Frank

# 11

# A Miracle in the Mud

### The 2019 Kentucky Service Trip

In the spring of 2019, I traveled to Jackson, Kentucky for the annual mission service trip to Appalachia that I ran. Our project for this trip would be one of the most difficult projects we would ever physically tackle, but one we were confident could be accomplished. The plan was to build a large chapel on "Magnificat Farm," the Catholic worker farm owned by Ellen and Josh. We had a planning meeting around Christmas with John Allen, who would be the mastermind of the actual construction of the chapel itself. He drew up a "detailed sketch of the plans" and provided me with a materials list and the estimated cost to purchase all we would need for the building. One of my tasks in the months that followed Christmas and our planning meeting was to find a way to raise the $20k that the project would ultimately cost when all the expenses of materials, travel and food were factored into the budget. Somehow God always provided the resources to make endeavors like this become a reality. Granted it wouldn't be as easy as going to God's ATM machine and taking out the needed funds, but rather talking to a number of generous benefactors who were willing to underwrite such a project as a way of bringing glory to their God.

Matt Fallon, our Director of Marist Youth and Marist Young Adults, was responsible for recruiting the young people that would be our workforce for the endeavor. By mid-spring, he had secured twelve young people who would join us for our work week in June. My usual cast of adults for such trips were again willing to make our annual pilgrimage of hope. Ed Kennedy, Maureen Hagan, Pat Hagan, Mark O'Grady, John Allen, Marcus Allen, Matt Fallon, Tim Hagan and Br. Brian Poulin had each been on many of our prior weeklong experiences in Appalachia. A few other adults also joined us for this trip as first timers, namely Kathy, Suzanne, and Jimmy Hagan.

A few weeks prior to the actual trip, Ed Kennedy and I flew down to Kentucky so that we could do some preliminary work and have the worksite ready when our crew would arrive. We rented a car at Lexington airport and drove about an hour to Jackson to meet Ellen and Josh. After we got settled at the church where we would be staying, we followed Ellen and Josh out to the farm which was about twenty minutes out from the town of Jackson. On our first day we walked up from their home to the potential site we would build the chapel. Our first task was to clear all the trees and brush that covered the area. We rented a small backhoe that would help us to eventually level the land after we finished clearing the space. The biggest task that we needed to accomplish on this short trip was to carefully layout the blueprint for the base of the chapel and install sixteen concrete footings that would be the foundation that the chapel would be built upon. The two days that followed were marked by heavy rain and made our tasks even more difficult, but thanks to Ed we were able to fly home content in knowing that the chapel had a good foundation to rest once it was built.

Early on the morning of Father's Day, our NY/NJ crew departed Roselle and drove our convoy of cars and vans the twelve hours to Jackson. Another car of young people drove down from Chicago while two students from Texas flew into Lexington for the trip. We all met at Holy Cross parish in Jackson and were warmly welcomed by Ellen and Josh. After a supper of pizza, we had a little orientation meeting and our first nightly prayer reflection. All were tired from the long trip and enjoyed an early night to bed.

After a 7:30 am simple breakfast, we assembled in the parish church for our morning prayer and then departed to Magnificat Farm to begin our workweek. My main job during the week was to provide the meals and be the gopher to get needed supplies for the worksite. Everyone else would have a physically much tougher week than I did. None of us had ever experienced the amount of rain that would constantly fall during our week in Kentucky. The biggest difficulty that was caused by the constant deluge was that it quickly turned the half mile dirt trail from Ellen and Josh's house up to the site of the chapel into a mudslide. Every piece of wood needed for the construction of the chapel would have to be carried up that hill by our group. The actual weight of all the needed wood was over ten thousand pounds. Imagine attempting to carry that amount of material up a steep, slick, muddy hill that got progressively worse by the minute.

John Allen and Ed Kennedy set up a large fifty-foot by fifty-foot tarp to cover the area of the chapel so that they could safely work and use the needed tools in the midst of the rain. Although the tarp did keep some of the water out, it also felt like a sauna underneath it. John Allen somehow worked his usual magic and made progress in securing the frame of the chapel. The team members who were carrying up the lumber soon became almost unrecognizable as each one was completely covered in Mud from head to toe.

What happened over the course of our five workdays there was nothing short of a "Miracle in the Mud." It would be difficult to convince an army to conquer the task of carrying all that heavy wood up a muddy trail for hours on end, yet our young people did it joyfully and with great enthusiasm, The only words that were not spoken during that entire trip were words of complaints or discontent. Our entire team sacrificed and gave all they had out of their love and admiration for Ellen and also in knowing that this beautiful chapel would be dedicated to St. Marcellin. When we finished construction on Friday, we held the first prayer service ever in the chapel and dedicated it. The tears of joy that each participant cried paralleled the rainfall that surrounded us. The chapel remains a living legacy to what young people can accomplish in only a few days. Next year we will return to the chapel to enclose the front and back of it with glass and stained glass. The young people that will participate next year will be walking on the shoulders of giants and hopefully not have to endure the mud and terrible weather.

Karem, Erin and Billy
Enjoying the mud

The work crew of the 2019   Miracle in the Mud

"It takes courage to grow up and become who you really are."

– *e. e. cummings*

# 12

## The Volunteers of the MBCE

The Marist Brothers Center in Esopus is devoted to the work of Christian evangelization. The MBCE is a "sacred space" and holy ground, where God's grace touches people in many different ways. It is "home" to over 5,000 young people annually who attend retreats, service opportunities as well as special needs camps during the summer months. As stated in its vision statement, "At the Marist Brothers Center in Esopus, the presence of God is discovered in a new way by young people and adults alike. Hearts are touched, lives changed and 'Jesus is made known and loved.'" Founded and administered by the Marist Brothers, a Roman Catholic religious order established for the Christian education of youth with special concern for the poor and marginalized, the Center offers experiences of community, service, and spiritual formation in a setting of great natural beauty."

I have been involved with the MBCE for almost forty years and it is one of the key foundational and spiritual cornerstones of my life. I began my connection to Esopus while in high school and through my college years as a place for school retreats and Marist Encounters, some fun service work weekends and as part of kitchen crews, maintenance crews and as a counselor at some of the special needs camps that are hosted at the MBCE each summer. I made lifelong friends and regardless of how tired I ever was at the end of a camp I always felt I left with so much more than I had given. Working in those camps continues to be a source of great inspiration and hope for me, although my involvement in recent years has been limited to only cooking for one of the ten camps. Each summer when I cook my favorite part of every day is sitting outside during mealtimes to watch the kitchen crew serve the food to all the campers and staff. Each of the special needs children at the camp show all of us a limitless and abundant amount of love and gratitude that is worth more than any words can describe.

What also has amazed me at every single one of these camps is the incredible loving and dedicated efforts shown by all the young people who serve as counselors at the camp and make the week such a gift to each child who attends. These counselors willingly do things every day that most people would never attempt in a lifetime. Some of these tasks include caring for teenagers with little motor skills who are confined to wheelchairs. Counselors are responsible for feeding, showering, and assisting these children to go to the bathroom and cleaning up after them when they make a mess which occur frequently. They are fearless and will lovingly embrace whatever challenges occur throughout the week, having the simple desire to ensure that the child they are caring for has a great experience. These campers have consistently expressed that their week at camp is the best week of their year.

In one of Jesus' parables, he teaches "The King will reply, 'Truly I tell you, whatever you did for one of the least of these brothers and sisters of mine, you did for me.'" (Matt 25:40 NIV). When I reflect on that scripture passage, I can't help but believe how proud God and Jesus are when they look down from heaven upon the many young people who serve as volunteers at the MBCE and who bring those words to reality on a daily basis.

Each year over seven hundred young people volunteer to work at the special needs camps at the MBCE and have been doing so for almost fifty years. Extraordinarily, there is always a waiting list of young people who want to volunteer at the camps but cannot because of a lack of space. Each of these volunteers that work the camps radically impacts the lives of the campers in a most profound and loving way.

Some of the young people who volunteer will work multiple weeks and do so for many years. Others have offered the gift of being full time volunteers for a period of one or two years. I have been blessed to have had the chance to get to know and at times live in community with some of our yearlong volunteers. Rob Costello, Nina Lokar, Rosie Mulligan, Luis Ramos, Tyler Pereira, Sean Harrison and Rob Dittus all continue to be an inspiration in my life and are examples of the astounding generosity young people are willing to contribute to the building up of the kingdom of God.

The spirit of community and generosity that has been created among the many volunteers of the MBCE is beyond remarkable and hard to even describe in words. A few examples of the amazing bonds of friendship, love and commitment that is shared among this unique community include: -

- A group of current and past MBCE volunteers who every two years take part in the Esopus century ride. This event which was begun in 2000 by Archbishop Molloy alumni Brad Katinas '90 and Ivan Kamin '88 to help raise needed funds for the MBCE has now raised over $200,000 and consistently attracts about twenty-five riders who make the one-hundred-mile cycle from NYC to Esopus. The riders collect sponsors for their efforts and are also supported by a large contingent of support cars who make the event possible and safe for the riders. Damian Schiano and Joe McMenamin have the distinction of being the only two Esopus century riders to have completed ten of the eleven century rides to date.

- On July 16, 2016, Sean Harrison, a longtime MBCE volunteer, was involved in a tragic accident on the Jackie Robinson parkway in NYC when a tree fell and crushed his car which resulted in him becoming paralyzed from the chest down for life. He had recently graduated from Mt. St. Mary's College in Newburgh with a degree in nursing. After the accident he spent many weeks in rehab trying to adjust to the realities of being confined to a wheelchair. His parents began the process of selling their family home so they could purchase a new house that would be handicap accessible. The process of selling the old house and finding the new one would not be a quick or easy endeavor and the question of where Sean should live in the interim became an urgent need. Br. Owen Ormsby, Mike Trainor and the other members of the MBCE staff and larger Esopus community immediately offered to welcome Sean to return "Home" to Esopus and to stay and be a full time MBCE volunteer for as long as was needed. Sean quickly moved in and became a vital part of the MBCE community for almost a year. He enriched the lives of all those he lived as well as all who came to the MBCE during that time period. He continues to be an important member of the MBCE and Marist family.

- In 2016, Allie Brennan, an Archbishop Molloy graduate and long-time MBCE volunteer, began Esopus Runners, an annual fundraiser to support the needs of the MBCE. This annual event has now raised over $100,000 through the hard work of a group of dedicated runners and their sponsors. This year's event had to be a virtual run as a result of the Covid-19 pandemic, but it became the largest one to date with the greatest number of participants and even a number of International Marists joining in the event.

- During the spring, summer and fall of 2020, the MBCE sadly had to cancel all retreats and camps as a result of the coronavirus. Many of the regular MBCE summer volunteers answered a greater call during this time in being first responders and essential workers on the front lines in NYC during the worst of the pandemic. The MBCE looks forward to being able to formally honor those heroes when it is safe to allow large groups to again gather at the MBCE. Members of the MBCE community, who were sadly lost to the coronavirus will likewise be appropriately remembered on a future date.

- Another sad but touching example of the incredible community that is created and shared by the MBCE volunteers happened this summer. Sae Suh had been a longtime and deeply loved volunteer at the MBCE. In the spring of 2020, he was diagnosed with stage four cancer and knew his time was limited. His main concern was that the cost of his needed medical treatment would have a devastating long-term effect on his wife and family. He did not want to die knowing that he would leave them with such a financial burden. The compassionate and loving response to this tragedy by Matt Waldron, Brendan Cloonan, Brian Davis and countless other MBCE volunteers was beyond heroic. Throughout the months that followed, this extended MBCE family responded to meet every possible need that Sae and his family would face. They helped raise over $120,000 to cover his medical and other bills, Many of the MBCE community who are nurses and doctors, helped provide extra hospice care in his final weeks and when Sae finally lost his brave battle to cancer on September 5th, his funeral expenses were immediately covered by his loving MBCE community members. While the loss of Sae, at the young age of 36, is heartbreaking, the witness and love of so many members of the MBCE family is heartwarming. Their example of responding to a friend in need is a lasting reminder of the many profound life lessons that being part of this MBCE community has on so many lives.

Students from around the USA
attend a LaValla weekend at the MBCE

The Peace and Serenity of Esopus

Members of the 2018 Esopus Runners

Matt Waldron, Sae Suh (R.7.P.) and Brendan CLoonan
during Kids 1 Camp in happier times.

"Few will have the greatness to bend history itself; but each of us can work to change a small portion of events, and in the total of all those acts will be written the history of this generation."

*– Robert F. Kennedy*

# 13

## Broadcasters of Hope

Another young person that continues to be an inspiration to me and a promise of hope in our world is K.C. Murray. He was one of our Marist Youth leaders during my days at Roselle Catholic and with Ed Kennedy was instrumental in helping layout the design of the RC labyrinth during the 2008 RC summer service days. K.C. also was one of the young people who traveled with me to Australia for the Marist International Youth Festival and the World Youth Days.

The United States Conference of Catholic Bishops developed a unique way to allow Catholics in the U.S.A. to share in some of the themes from what would take place at the WYD in Sydney. They offered the opportunity for ten young people from all across the United States, who were going to attend WYD, to apply to be National Youth Reporters for the USCCB. The application process involved each applicant writing an essay explaining how as a young person they wanted to share the Good News and why they were a worthy candidate to be chosen. More than one thousand young people applied to be selected as National Youth Reporters to cover the upcoming WYD events. K.C. Murray and Megan Friedman, a classmate and fellow RC Marist Youth leader, both applied and were chosen to represent the United States as youth reporters.

I traveled down to Washington D.C. with them to attend the training workshop, where they received all their necessary press credentials as well as tape recorders and small video cameras to record the interviews that they would need to do each day during both the Marist International Festival and the WYD. Both of them hit it out of the park as reporters and many of their stories attracted the largest followings and were shared nationally and internationally.

After studying environmental science at Rutgers's University, K.C. joined the United States Peace Corps, where he lived and worked in the jungles of Panama in a village called Ngäbe, which was a two-hour boat ride from the nearest road, store or health clinic. He helped the local tribal people learn about and build clean water systems, build latrines and improve the quality of their lives and increase their life expectancy by decreasing their exposure to many diseases to which they had been vulnerable. After Panama, he worked for the World Health Organization in Geneva where he did research for their cardiovascular disease group. He next spent two years in Equatorial Guinea where he managed a malaria surveillance program for the country. In one three-month period, he hired 40 staff members to assist him in testing approximately 15,000 individuals. During that testing, his team diagnosed 1,522 malaria cases and treated them on-site. He also managed a team that trained children how to use mosquito nets. K.C. recently got engaged and is back living in New Jersey. He continues to reach out offering to help foster the Marist mission in any way he can.

Each year our USA Marist schools, as a way of being in solidarity as a Marist Family, work together to raise awareness and needed funds for various Marist projects around the globe. This past year our schools helped educate all their young people about the many issues and difficulties that so many refugees and migrants face each day. The schools also shared videos of numerous Marist projects that are assisting many of the world's refugees and migrants and raised needed funds to support those projects. Next year, our schools will be focusing on our "Common Home" and the many environmental issues facing our planet. K.C. has already agreed to be a featured speaker at a national Marist conference we will host in the fall for selected Marist Youth leaders from all our schools. They will return from the conference as ambassadors to their schools to help promote next year's Marist solidarity efforts. He and two other prominent presenters will help educate the participants at the conference about many global environmental issues and concerns as well as offer suggestions of things that might be achieved at a local level by our schools to help alleviate some of these problems.

It is always rewarding to know that so many of our young people who impacted our world when they were in high school continue to live those same values as they journey through life and still live the gospel in remarkable ways. Both KC and Megan were exceptional youth leaders and highly committed to serving the least favorite through the RC Bridges program, the annual West Virginia service trips and the RC summer service days as well as being Broadcasters of Hope to the entire catholic world during those WYD in Sydney. As their lives continued, they have never stopped being examples of people that are a living gospel in our world.

Megan and K.C. our USA National Ambassadors to WYD

Our RC Marist Youth Group at WYD

"One child, one teacher, one book, one pen can change the world."

– *Malala Yousafzai*

# 14
## A Shining Light

I first met Opal Vadhan when she was a freshman in college and actively involved in our Marist Young Adult program. She was a recent graduate of Archbishop Molloy high school and had been very active in the school's campus ministry and Marist Youth activities while in high school. I met her on a Marist Encounter retreat in Esopus. She was a leader for one of the retreat discussion groups which is a major part of the retreat. I was the adult presence in her group. I had worked on many Encounter retreats over the years and her leadership skills and gifts in running the group were among the best I had ever observed. She also gave a remarkable talk on prayer. One of the things I liked most about her was that she was a young Hindu woman not afraid to share her own faith but also embraced many of the teachings of both the gospel and our Marist charism. In a world that has too much division, I was grateful that someone from a different faith background was such an active member of our Marist Young Adult program. She was someone that many younger people looked up to because she passionately lived her life in a way that always centered on helping others, especially the least favored.

While on that retreat, I gave a talk about how young people can truly make a difference in the world. As part of the talk, I showed clips from the video of Malala's United Nations speech and shared about what Ellen Salmi was doing at the time as a Marist volunteer in Senegal, Africa. After the talk, Opal asked me about what possibilities there might be for her to do something like Ellen in being a Marist Volunteer. She said she would be willing to spend her summer as a volunteer overseas if there was a need. We kept in touch and I connected her with the Marist Missionary Sisters as I had done with Ellen. During that next summer, Opal spent her vacation living and working with the Sisters on the island of Jamaica. She worked in an outreach program for homeless children and did an amazing job. The experience of those children in her life had a profound and lasting effect on her. When she returned from her summer of volunteering, she began a social media campaign to raise needed funds for the programs that helped those children. Her fundraising efforts were highly successful and greatly impacted the lives of many children. She made another return trip back to Jamaica to offer further assistance.

While in college she continued to stay very active as a Marist Young Adult working on Encounters and Marist Youth Gatherings every year. She also worked for one semester as an intern at the White House under President Obama. Upon graduating from college, she was hired on the advance team for Hillary for America, which was Hillary Clinton's 2016 Campaign for President of the United States. And after the election, she's stayed on with Hillary Clinton as her executive assistant. She continues to be a prominent speaker at numerous Marist events as well as various conferences, she is passionate about continuing to help women and children. During the recent Covid-19 pandemic, when NYC was hit the hardest, she became a full-time volunteer with World Central Kitchen, a food relief organization that helps distribute thousands of meals each day to those most in need. The organization has served over 7 million meals in New York and New Jersey during COVID. She remains a shining light in a sometimes very dark world.

Sometimes in life, we never know the impact our lives can have on another person. I shared Ellen's story of her volunteerism on a retreat and it inspired Opal to follow in the same footsteps as Ellen and find an opportunity to serve the least favored in our world. So many young people are quietly living the gospel in dramatic ways. When other young people hear about such possibilities, they too begin to search for ways that they might likewise positively impact the lives of those in need. They just need to be given some options as to how they might achieve such dreams and aspirations.

Opal with some of the children in Jamaica

Opal pictured with Nobel Peace Prize winner Malaya Yousafzai

"What lies behind us, and what lies before us are but tiny matters compared to what lies within us."

*– Ralph Waldo Emerson*

# 15

## The Big Fella

Matt Fallon at first glance might be a rather intimidating figure standing at over 6' 8" in height, but it doesn't take long to realize he is a gentle giant. Matt is a 2002 graduate of Roselle Catholic and as a student attended the very first Marist Youth Gathering at Marist College in 2000. After high school he became very active in the recently formed Marist Young Adult program and would serve in various roles at Marist Encounters and future Marist Youth Gatherings. He became the first chairperson of the Marist Young Adult National Advisory committee.

After graduating from Catholic University, he spent a year as a Capuchin volunteer where he lived in community and helped run retreats for many young people. After his volunteer year, he began his teaching career at Christopher Columbus high school in Miami, one of our USA Marist schools. He became a solid and inspiring teacher and also helped with the school's Marist Youth group. After five years at Columbus, he was asked by our USA Province to become the Director of Operations for the MBCE. He did a great job in this position and as a result the Province asked him to once again change roles and become the Director of Marist Youth and the Director of Marist Young Adults for the USA Province. As part of his current position, he has led many young people on pilgrimages to places of our Marist roots in France, attended several Marist International festivals with our young adults and has attended numerous international meetings around the world to represent our Province in the areas of Marist Youth, evangelization and Lay Marist formation. He has been a prominent speaker and presenter at many other National gatherings including the NCEA National convention.

Throughout his entire life since being a freshman at Roselle Catholic, he has embodied everything that is Marist and is a shining example for young people of how a young person can remain active in his or her faith at every stage of life. Matt doesn't just talk the talk, but honestly and deeply walks the walk as well. When the story of how the Marist charism impacted the lives of young people in our country during this century is someday told, Matt Fallon will be one of the reasons that impact became a reality.

Matt has become a close friend over these last twenty years and we have enjoyed some amazing times on vacations as well as in ministry together, Trips to Ireland, Hawaii and Alaska were among some of the most memorable holidays in my life and experiences like the "Miracle in the Mud," "LaValla Weekends," pilgrimages to France are some of the best highlights in my life as a Marist Brother.

One of my favorite memories of being with Matt was on one of our pilgrimages to France. We arrived into Lyon airport with about a dozen fellow Marists in our group. I rented a stick shift van for our week and after we collected our bags and headed to the nearby city of Lyon. On top of a steep hill overlooking the old part of the city is the cathedral of Fourvière, which is the site of where St. Marcellin Champagnat, Venerable Jean-Claude Colin and a few other newly ordained priests pledged to one day create a society in honor of Mary. That pledge would be the beginning of the eventual establishment of the four different branches of the Marist family, namely the Marist Fathers, Marist Brothers, Marist Sisters and Marist Missionary Sisters.

When we arrived in the city, we could easily see in the distance the statue of Our Lady of Fourvière which overlooked the city. Not having a GPS, we self-navigated our way toward the shrine. As we drew closer to our destination the road we were travelling on began to steeply go uphill and grow increasingly narrower. As we continued to climb, we began to encounter and drive over a series of steps, but it was actually a road as cars were parked all along this narrow road. Trying to navigate our way up became more and more interesting as we had about two inches of space on either side of the van. It seemed like every other car on the road was either a Mini Cooper or a one-person Smart Car, not an over-sized van. To make matters worse there was now a string of about ten cars following our van up this hill with the car directly behind us annoyingly only inches from our rear bumper. Trying to navigate a stick shift van on a steep hill without ever rolling back tested all my driving abilities. Next came the most challenging of all as the road came to a V-shaped turn. It was geometrically impossible for the van to make such a turn. The only remaining option was to drive up to the very end of the V and then drive up the remaining part of the hill in reverse. As luck would have it this last segment went around a sharp turn. Matt at this point was out of the vehicle and walking up the hill to direct me as I slowly proceeded backwards. When I looked out my front window, my friend in the immediate car following us up the hill was now about three inches from my front bumper and screaming obscenities at me in French. I finally made it around the final bend to discover that this road exited onto a major roadway. Matt had to go out on the roadway and stop all traffic in order for us to safely make it. We still laugh when we recall how we travelled up a narrow road backwards to get to that sacred shrine. I think I prayed more on the ride up the hill than I actually did when we got to the chapel.

We had many ridiculous adventures like the one I just described, and Matt was always a calming and encouraging presence and would say, "No worries, we got this Dano." I pray that the next generation of Marist Youth might follow such a path and live such an authentic Christian and Marist life as Matt continues to do.

Matt Fallon, Tim Hagan and Br. Todd with a group of
Marist Young Adults in LaValla, France

Matt leading morning prayer on the Hudson River in
Esopus

"Never doubt that a small group of thoughtful, committed people can change the world. Indeed, it is the only thing that ever has."

*– Margaret Mead*

# 16

## Blue Mission

Another shining example of a former Marist student who continues to live our Marist charism and significantly impact the world is Danny Rodriguez, who graduated from Christopher Columbus High School in Miami. While Danny was still in high school, he went on a service trip to the Dominican Republic and witnessed first-hand the devastating poverty most of the people in that country had to endure. He made up his mind, as a result of that trip, that he would dedicate his life to help alleviate such situations. He continued to go on similar service trips as he made his way through college. His college studies gave him the necessary knowledge to create a non-profit organization dedicated to helping many rural people in areas such as Dominican Republic to obtain two of the most basic necessities for life, namely water and bathrooms.

Danny founded Blue Missions in 2010 and its "Be Bold Model" of operation is very unique. Danny and his team provide the expertise and allow school, church and other faith-based volunteer groups to help rural villages to obtain clean water and install sanitation systems for those villages. The volunteer groups raise money to cover the cost of their flights and the needed piping and materials to complete the project in a particular village. One hundred percent of their fundraising is utilized for that project with no money used for administrative costs such as covering the salaries of Danny and his team. The team does its own fundraising and the yearly sponsorship they raise covers all such administrative costs.

In the ten years since Blue Missions was founded almost twenty-five thousand people now have clean drinking water and almost six thousand people are connected with proper sanitation. More than three thousand volunteers have participated in volunteer trips with Blue Missions. One of our younger Brothers recently completed his master's degree which required him to work in a third world country and study ways of impacting and improving the quality of life for poor communities. Br. Brian spent that semester living in Dominican Republic working as part of the team for Blue Missions.

Danny was twenty-two when he established the company. Its mission continues to evolve as they have recently expanded their efforts to now impact rural villages in several other Caribbean and Central American countries. Many of our schools have sent volunteer groups to be one of the many teams that bring these life changing results to some of the poorest villages in the world. Matt Fallon has likewise coordinated groups of Marist Young Adults to avail themselves of this opportunity to make the Gospel come to life in such a real and meaningful manner.

Danny has been a keynote speaker at a number of Marist Youth Conferences and is an impressive witness and inspiration to the youth of today of just how much difference a young person can make in the world if they have the vision and fortitude to make those ambitions come true.

I am incredibly hopeful that our country and world has a brighter future because of young people like Danny who have not sold out to the many mixed messages that are too often fed to young people regarding what it means to be successful in life. There are many people that are deemed successful simply by the criteria of how much money they make annually or the location of their summer home. Young people like Danny will probably never make it onto the Forbes list of wealthiest people, but when it comes to leaving a legacy of how one has impacted the lives of the most vulnerable in our world, I have no doubt that young people like Danny have a pretty good chance of being on such a list. My Dad often said that he had never seen a funeral hearse with a trailer carrying one's life possessions following it. The only things in life that are really worth accumulating are loving relationships and the trail of good works that we leave behind.

Danny Rodriguez, CEO and Co-Founder of Blue Missions

"Our youth are not failing the system; the system is failing our youth. Ironically, the very youth who are being treated the worst are the young people who are going to lead us out of this nightmare."

– *Rachel Jackson*

# 17

## Saying "Yes"

After I left Roselle Catholic in 2011, I spent four enjoyable years working as one of the Vocation Directors for the USA Province. I spent most of my days visiting our schools, actively being involved in youth retreats and other types of youth gatherings where I would both promote the Marist Brothers as a vocation option for young men to consider as well as challenge all young people to discern on how they might to choose to share the gift of their lives in responding to God's call.

During those years I had the opportunity to get to know a promising young man by the name of Luis Ramos. He was a recent graduate of Mountt. St. Michael Academy, our Marist school in the Bronx. Like many other former Marist Youth kids, he became very active in our Marist Young Adult program during his college years. He was a very spiritual person, articulate in sharing his faith and totally embraced the Marist charism. As his years in college passed, we worked together on many programs such as Marist Encounters, LaValla Weekends, and Marist Youth Gatherings. He became the national chairperson of the Marist Young Adult community and worked closely with Matt Fallon to help bring the program to a new level by engaging more social media as a way to connect this 21st century community. As a result of his extensive work in Marist programs he felt called to convert to Catholicism and entered the RCIA program at Iona college, where he attended school. His family were very religious, and his dad was a pastor of an evangelical church. They fully embraced his decision to choose which religion would allow him to best live his faith.

Luis traveled with me on two pilgrimages during this time period. The first was to attend the Marist International Festival and World Youth Days held in Brazil. The theme of that Marist gathering was "CHANGE." Participants were challenged to be the needed change in the world as the future rested on their shoulders and ultimately on their willingness to respond "Yes" to God's call in their lives. The second pilgrimage was to France to explore our Marist foundations and re-live the early stories of our Founder and Marist history. The pilgrimage to France helped Luis decide to commit to be a yearlong volunteer at the MBCE after his graduation.

Luis' year in Esopus allowed him to share his many gifts and deep faith life with the thousands of young people that passed through the MBCE that year for retreats and camps. As a result of his volunteer experience, he felt God was calling him to live his Marist call in an even deeper and more profound way by entering the formation program of our province and becoming a postulant. He spent his postulancy year at the St. Barnabas community in the Bronx before entering our Novitiate on the campus of Marist college. He spent six weeks of his novitiate with other Marist novices from the Marist Brothers' Arco-Norte Region at our international novitiate in Colombia. I had the chance to visit him at the novitiate in Colombia and it was incredibly hopeful to watch Luis and twelve other young Marist Brothers enjoy being together as they came to deepen their understanding of our history and Marist brotherhood. As I watched these young brothers, I easily imagined how Champagnat may have felt with his early young recruits as he prepared them to be the future and carry the Marist dream forward. I also reflected on how there were more young brothers present in Colombia then there was in the entire order during those early years when Champagnat began the Marist Brothers. If a handful of Marcellin's recruits could help shape a dream that has lasted more than two hundred years and has impacted countless lives, how can we not be anything but hopeful in having such fine young Brothers of today to likewise carry on the dream and torch?

After he completed his two-year novitiate, he professed his first vows on August 15th, 2019. This past year, he joined Br. Sam Amos, another of our younger brothers, as a teacher at Marist High School in Chicago. Hopefully schools will be able to re-open in the fall with the uncertainty of the corona virus. When Marist High School does re-open, the Marist community in Chicago will get to witness, at their first school-wide Mass, the vow ceremony of two young Brothers. Luis will renew his vows as a temporary professed brother and Sam will make his final vows as a Marist Brother.

There are about one hundred young men around our Marist world that are currently in formation to become Marist Brothers. When Champagnat died in 1840, there were less than two hundred total Marist Brothers in the entire congregation. Who is to say that the best and most productive years of Marist life are not still ahead of us?

I again emphasize how young people can leave a legacy that others will be inspired to follow. Opal became a missionary volunteer as a result of hearing Ellen's story. Rob Dittus, who was a full time volunteer this year at the MBCE, will now follow in Luis' footsteps and enter our postulancy this fall. May God continue to bless his Marist journey and the journey of all young men who say "Yes" to the call of Marist Brotherhood.

Our USA Marist Youth in Brazil. Br. Luis Ramos was one of our participants

Br. Luis on the occasion of his first profession of vows

"Our deepest fear is not that we are inadequate. Our deepest fear is that we are powerful beyond measure. It is our light, not our darkness that most frightens us. We ask ourselves, Who am I to be brilliant, gorgeous, talented, fabulous? Actually, who are you not to be? You are a child of God. Your playing small does not serve the world. There is nothing enlightened about shrinking so that other people won't feel insecure around you. We are all meant to shine, as children do. We were born to make manifest the glory of God that is within us. It is not just in some of us; it is in everyone. And as we let our own light shine, we unconsciously give other people permission to do the same. As we are liberated from our own fear, our presence automatically liberates others."

*– Marianne Williamson, as written for Nelson Mandela.*

# 18

## Living on Borrowed Time

I grew up in an Irish-American household as both of my parents immigrated from Ireland in the 1950's. My mom worked for Pan American Airways which allowed our family frequent opportunities to visit all our family in Ireland. My dad was from County Cork and my mom was from County Cavan. I was very fortunate as a young child to spend so much time with all my uncles, aunts and cousins in Ireland as those experiences are among my most treasured memories in life. Two of my cousins in Cavan, who were a few years younger than me, were born with cystic fibrosis. Bernie and Eileen were amazing children. They had very difficult childhoods as they spent weeks and even months each year at the Crumlin Children's Hospital in Dublin getting treatments for this terrible disease. I didn't realize or comprehend the seriousness of their illness until I was in my teenage years.

My best memories of Bernie and Eileen as young girls was watching them do Irish step dancing around the fire of my Uncle Jimmy's house. My worst memories were the many times we stopped at Crumlin Hospital to visit them during their many stays. Eileen died from the disease in March of 1983 at the age 11. I couldn't believe it and began to realize that Bernie would one day face the same fate as there was no cure for this disease and treatments in those days were not as advanced or successful as they are in more recent times.

As the next few years passed, I grew to have a much deeper appreciation and empathy for the strength of character that Bernie, her parents and two older siblings each had. They lived each day hoping and praying for a miracle but knew that without one, Bernie was on borrowed time. She continued to need frequent stays in the hospital and eventually had to stop Irish dancing as her weakened lungs could no longer handle the stress.

I really enjoyed my time with her over the next few years as she grew into an amazing teenager and young woman. She loved much of the same music I enjoyed such as Bruce Springsteen and was a fashion queen whom my mom loved to spoil with new outfits. She had an uplifting personality and was always filled with hope. Her faith life was far deeper than mine. She volunteered every year to go to Lourdes and assist people in wheelchairs. She would say that they had it much worse than she did. She shared about how when she would bring them up close to the famous grotto at Lourdes to pray for a needed miracle. She would ask Mary to grant them their requests and if there were any miracles to spare, she could use one herself.

When she finished high school, she began working as a teacher's assistant in Cavan town for the children of itinerants (Irish gypsies). She loved her job and was great at it. It also made her feel independent and gave her a real sense of purpose in life as she knew she was making a difference each day in the lives of these younger children. Her older brother PJ, who was working in New York by this stage sent her the money to by herself a car. It was probably the greatest present she ever got. It really allowed her to feel like other young people her age and not always be dependent on others. Her condition began to get worse and she eventually needed to be on oxygen full time, but it never stopped her from going to work or Mass. Her dad worried that people might laugh at her and told her if she wanted to stay home it would be OK. She would hear nothing of it and said she was proud to live her faith and if people had a problem with her oxygen tank, they would just have to get over it.

The miracle never came, and Bernie was lost to us at the far too young age of twenty-three. Her funeral was something few people will ever experience. Yes, the crowd was huge as one might expect for a young person's funeral, but what was really a testament to her life was the fact that every itinerant family in Cavan paid their respects to her for the kindness and love she brought into their children's lives. Those same children were there too, weeping and mourning for an incredibly special friend. Bernie impacted more lives in her short twenty-three years with us than many people will in a lifetime of eighty or more years.

Attitude is everything. If I had to live when I was young as Bernie did knowing I was on borrowed time, I don't believe my main focus would have been on how I can help others in the time I have left as she did. I would have been angry and could never have handled an illness with the grace she displayed, no matter what challenges or sufferings she faced on a given day. She will always remain a shining star in the hearts of all of us that loved her and still miss her enduring smile and laughter. Both her parents have since joined her and Eileen in heaven, but her loving brother and sister, Pj and Mairead, keep her legacy alive and have passed on her amazing loving spirit to their own children.

Bernie pictured at her 21st birthday celebration

"Dear Young People, do not bury your talents, the gifts that God has given you! Do not be afraid to dream of great things."

*– Pope Francis*

# 19

## Every Vote Counted

On January 2, 2017, the Marist Brothers celebrated the 200th Anniversary of St. Marcellin Champagnat's founding of the Institute in the small hamlet of LaValla, France. As the anniversary date grew closer, all parts of the Institute reflected on appropriate ways to commemorate the special occasion. The Provincial Council of our USA Province likewise planned potential ways to mark this event in our Marist history. While individual schools were encouraged to hold special masses or prayer services for their local communities, the Council decided on a unique way that we as a Province might celebrate. Some folks in the Province made numerous suggestions such as holding a Province Mass and asking representatives from all our ministries and communities to attend. The Council discerned that, because the main focus of our Marist mission was always on the evangelization of young people, our keynote event should have a similar emphasis.

We as a worldwide Marist institute and as the USA Province firmly believe in the potential of young people to change the world. The Council declared March 29th, 2017 to be a Marist National Day of Service. Every Marist ministry and community around the USA were invited to find creative ways to engage all members of their local Marist communities to make a significant difference in their local worlds through service on this day. Some of us on the Council had shared about the success of similar types of events on a smaller scale like the Roselle Catholic summer service days and how such experiences not only helped the lives of many in a local community, but also greatly enriched the lives of those providing the service.

Our ministries rose to the occasion and were fully on board with making Marist National Day of Service a reality in the life of our province. Two creative additions were included to help enhance the experience of all the young people across our province that would participate. The first was a concept developed by Kevin Brady, a generous benefactor to a number of our ministries. He proposed reaching out to other benefactors to raise a significant amount of money that would be set aside to support the works of worthwhile global Marist projects. The allocation of how the money gets divided could be voted on by the students providing service in their local Marist communities so that their experience would also impact the wider Marist world.

We contacted our International Office of Solidarity in Rome (FMSI) to find out about potential Marist projects in need of funding that might fit into our plans. Five such Marist projects were selected; Our work with refugees with our Blue Marist community in Aleppo, Syria and our Fratelli project in Lebanon, our helping Displaced and Vulnerable Children in both Guatemala and the Congo and in support of the Blue Missions which brings clean water to rural villages in the Dominican Republic.

As a way of promoting the event a group of Marist Youth leaders from each Marist school around the country attended a special "LaValla Weekend" in early March to become ambassadors of the Marist National Day of Service. The weekend was informative in helping the students to understand the practical elements of what would take place on March 29th, and also was very impactful and facilitated the students to gain a clearer appreciation of why such a day was needed. One of the keynote speakers that weekend was the Hallack family, who had lived in Aleppo and were part of our Blue Marist community in the middle of that war zone. They shared with all of us on that weekend the lived realities of their lives and the lives of our fellow Marists in this war-torn country. As a result of the weekend, all the students returned to their respective schools. They would be speakers during prayer services back at their schools at the conclusion of the Marist National Day of Service and share with their fellow students how our efforts that day will also impact our global Marist world. Each Marist student around the USA would have a voice in determining how the monies would be allocated to the five global projects. We as a Province wanted to give our young people the power to make those decisions a reality. The idea was that at the end of Marist National Day of Service each student would log onto our Province website and vote for which projects would receive the most money by simply ranking the projects. The project with the most votes would receive fifty percent, second place twenty percent, third place fifteen percent, fourth place ten percent and fifth place five percent of the collected monies.

For the five weeks leading up to Marist National Day of Service a series of videos were produced and were shown to all students in our schools across the country. The five individual videos highlighted each of the five global projects that would be funded.

One of our schools decided as part of Marist National Day of Service that they would utilize their entire junior class on that day to prepare ten thousand meals for hungry children through the Feed My Starving Children program. This organization provided all the materials that the students would need to individually package the meals as well as the tractor trailer that would drive the container of food to a waiting ship so it could be delivered to those in need. Patrick Meyer, one of the campus ministers at the school, found a creative way to raise the needed funds to allow their junior class to accomplish their goal on that day. He asked for sponsors as he set out to break the Guinness Book of World Records for swinging on a playground swing, which was set up at the high school. The story gained traction at the local TV and media outlets who in turn covered the event as he attempted and broke the world record after swinging for 36 hours straight. His achievement received much playtime as did the reason why he attempted the record.

On March 29, 2017 the Marist National Day of Service was a huge success. Every local Marist community around the country provided needed works in their local communities. The day concluded with all communities joining in a prayer that featured a live video from the Br. Pat McNamara, our USA Provincial, thanking them for their work that day and reminding them to cast their votes before midnight for their choices of which global projects they felt were most important at this time.

The only unexpected consequence of the entire day was the results of the actual voting. Somehow each of the five projects received almost the exact number of votes from more than six thousand students. Another surprise was that most of the students not only completed the voting but took the time to respond to a question about how the experience of Marist National Day of Service was for them. Their collective responses were all similar and almost unbelievable. They loved the day, hoped it would happen again, but felt that it was totally unfair to ask them to choose between the five projects in regard to which ones were the most important and should receive the greater funding. They overwhelmingly responded that all the Marist Projects were equally important, and they wanted all the projects to receive the same amount of money. Their collective response was heard, and the allocation of the funds was correctly changed to ensure all projects received the same amounts. Our USA young people have truly come to know the true measure on what it means to be Marist.

DOING 03
GOOD
IS GOOD 29
TO DO
MARIST
NATIONAL 17
DAY OF
SERVICE

World Record holder, Pat Meyer, swings to raise money to support Feeding My Hungry Children

"Unless someone like you cares a whole awful lot, nothing is going to get better.  It's not."

– *Dr. Seuss*

# 20

## Where it all Began

I graduated from University College Cork in Ireland in 1989. While in college I enjoyed playing hurling with many of the best athletes ever to play the game. I was blessed to have been coached by Fr. Michael O'Brien, who was a legend and led our college teams to unparalleled success. I was convinced by a friend to pursue a Higher Degree in Education which is the Irish equivalent of a teacher's certification. Although I never thought I would end up being a teacher, it would allow me the possibility to remain involved with the team for an additional year. As part of the program, I taught math at Presentation Secondary School in Ballyphehane, which was in one of the toughest areas of Cork City. It was an all-girls high school.

By the end of the first week of teaching, I knew I had found my career choice as I fell in love with the possibility of impacting young lives just as many of my high school mentors and coaches had influenced mine. I visited the school's staff coffee room only once during the opening weeks of school and decided never to return. All that the teachers that were in there did was bemoan how horrible the girls in the school were and how they hated their jobs. The principal, who was a nun, didn't seem much better. Her only interest was looking after the girls that would academically succeed and bring honor to the school by how well they performed on Ireland's Leaving Certificate exams held at the end of their last year of school. Students that struggled or had other interests beside academics were merely tolerated at best. The school was lucky to have three great educators: Mrs. Geary, who was the assistant principal, Bob Mortell, who was the school's art teacher and Sr. Anne, a young nun, who taught geography and who I knew from college. They deeply cared for each student at the school as a person and wanted each one of them to succeed in life regardless of their academic abilities. Needless to say, Mrs. Geary, Bob and Sr. Anne were the colleagues with whom I would befriend.

My freshman students quickly realized that the principal and many of the staff of the school did not respect or like them very much. As the year progressed, I grew close to the students in the class and tried to assist them if possible, by simply being a listening ear. The Irish school system at that point had no such thing as guidance counselors to help young people to deal with the everyday ups and downs of life. The only guidance offered in any school at that time was in regard to filling out forms for state exams or information about how many points were needed for a student to get accepted into a college for a particular course of study.

During the month of December, the city of Cork announced a special charity day with the intention of raising needed funds for local charities. Teams, businesses, schools and churches were encouraged to do their part in helping many local people in need. One day in class the topic of the upcoming charity day came up and the students felt bad that the principal would never allow the students to miss precious class time for such a cause. As we continued to chat about the situation, I challenged the students to come up with a potential fundraiser the school might do and if it seemed acceptable, I would try to find a way to make it happen. By the next time we met for class, they had their plan of action. The school was located a short distance from a famous lake in the city, named "The Lough," which had a nice walking trail around and was a place where many locals went to feed the birds and ducks that lived there. It was a natural bird sanctuary. They proposed bringing the entire school to "The Lough" to have them join hands around the circumference of the lake as a sign of solidarity for the many homeless and needy people in the city. As is often done in Ireland, another group of students and faculty could simultaneously be on the surrounding roadways with baskets to collect donations from passing cars. Their idea seemed brilliant and would be simple enough to implement. Presenting it to the principal was a waste of time as she would never even consider it, so I took the idea to Mrs. Geary, Bob and Anne. They loved it and helped me devise a way to make it happen. I had a few contacts at the city's newspaper from my involvement with the UCC hurling team and they agreed to give the event press coverage. "Hands around the Lough" raised almost fifteen hundred euro for our less fortunate brothers and sisters living on the streets. The newspaper offered a nice story and picture of the event on the front cover of the paper and my young students felt like they had just won an Olympic medal having achieved what they thought was impossible.

I was sad when our year ended. These young students truly impacted my life forever as they were the ones who fortified my deep passion for working with young people. Had it not been for them, I might never have continued on my path to the Marist Brothers. I can't imagine what the last thirty years of my life would have been had I gone down a different road. I am so grateful for the many graces and incredible people that have been part of my Marist journey.

I stayed in touch with that class throughout the remainder of their high school years and am still in touch with Finola and Rose, who even visited me in New York. I deeply regret that most young people in Ireland do not have the same opportunities during their years at school for retreats and service experiences like our Marist students do here in the USA. I know this through the realities of my many young cousins whom I am close to and see every year. Those children are among the most loving, kind and grateful of any children I have ever known and deserve so much more from their educational experience.

My first math class in Ballyphehane, Cork

"Modern man listens more willingly to witnesses than to teachers, and if he does listen to teachers, it is because they are witnesses."

*– Pope John VI*

# 21

## The A Team

Over the past 30 years, I have had the gift to be part of more than one hundred mission service trips with incredible young people who helped make many miracles happen for people with real needs and hardships. Each of those young people who attended any of these trips would give up their spring break vacations or weeks of their summer. They would also help raise the needed money to cover the cost of the trip and often the expense of the building supplies needed to complete a particular project. Words will never express the joy and gratitude that so many of our project recipients had for the profound impact that those endeavors had on their lives and the lives of their families.

While none of these projects could have ever been completed without those amazing young people who performed this labor of love, the projects themselves could never have even been attempted had it not been for another group of gifted and unselfish individuals. My role on these service trips is usually that of cooking for our volunteer group and driving to stores for needed supplies for the various work sites on any given day. The real unsung heroes are a group of people who are both the brain trust behind any project we attempt as well as the deeper reason these experiences remain powerful life lessons for the young people who participate in any one of our trips.

This team of humble but gifted individuals who have donated their time, expertise and hard work for many of these mission trips include:

- John Allen, a graduate of Roselle Catholic, a general contractor by trade and a master craftsman. John is a quiet unassuming hero who has helped design, oversee and construct more projects than I can remember. These projects have included roofing houses, building handicap ramps, handicap bathrooms, building decks and his masterpiece chapel in the woods of Magnificat Farm during the "Miracle in the Mud." Simply stated, John is the reason many of our projects were able to be attempted as he not only had the expertise and knowledge to undertake such tasks, but also provided all the necessary equipment and tools to make them become a reality.

- Marcus Allen, a graduate of Roselle Catholic and John's son. Marcus grew up learning his carpentry craft and skillset from his dad and spent a year after high school working for Habitat for Humanity. During his time as a project manager with Habitat, he developed a great ability to oversee volunteer groups and coordinate how to best utilize their skill level and integrate them safely into helping complete a particular work project. Marcus has been an invaluable asset to so many of our mission trips. Most of the young people who come on these service weeks had never used a power tool or even a hammer in their lives prior to the trip. Marcus patiently teaches them how to perform the needed tasks and enables them by the end of the week to feel incredible pride in having helped build and complete the project.

- Ed Kennedy, a parent of three Roselle Catholic alumni and a landscaper by trade is a "Jack of all trades." He has worked in everything from tree cutting to his current role as the Director of Outdoor Adventure for the Marist Brothers Center in Esopus. Ed has designed and overseen some of the most memorable projects, we have ever attempted including the building of both the Roselle Catholic and MBCE Labyrinths and the outdoor chapel in Esopus. He has been part of numerous West Virginia and Kentucky mission trips and has greatly impacted the lives of all the young people who have been part of those trips. One family in West Virginia still remembers him lovingly as they continue to enjoy their "Ed Kennedy Deck."

- Maureen Hagan, a former campus minister at Roselle Catholic and the current Director of Marist Lay Formation for the USA Province has been the spiritual backbone of many of these trips. She not only provides creative, reflective and rich morning and evening prayers each day of the trip but always provides an amazing nurturing motherly spirit to the young people. While the work projects are always an important element of each trip, the main hope is that the entire experience will be a life changing and memorable encounter in the faith life of each young person who is part of any particular mission trip team. Thanks to Maureen and her deeply spiritual insights that goal is always achieved.

- Pat Hagan, former Roselle Catholic educator and coach, has provided a deep witness to many young people on how to live our Marist characteristics including the ability to "do good quietly" as well as live "family spirit." He has been an incredible role model to our young people and continually shows them that it is OK to work hard and that it is a gift to be a loving husband, father and friend to all.

- Denny Beiter, a parent of six Bishop Donahue graduates, was a guardian angel for many of our mission trips. He is one of the most faith filled friends I have ever known and was always willing to offer his wide skill set in helping make many a project become a reality. Most of those projects were in the rural hollows of southern West Virginia.

- Marcus O'Grady, another Roselle Catholic alum and now a retired New Jersey firefighter has been a constant presence on our annual Appalachian mission trips. While he always takes the lead in helping to break down structures in disrepair, he also is a great reminder to all young people that no matter what job they may choose in life, they can always find ways to give back and make a difference in their community.

- Tomas O'Riordan, a cousin and current Director of Facilities at the Marist Brothers Center in Esopus, has been an instrumental support to so many of our projects and undertakings over the years. When I worked in West Virginia, he not only financially supported many of our needs but also visited frequently to offer moral and hands-on support. He likewise has financially supported our annual Esopus Runners campaign and has joined us on mission trips as well. His current role in Esopus allows him to utilize his wide range of skills to help the MBCE Team allow many young people to volunteer and keep that great mission going strong.

- Br. Owen Ormsby, quietly supported and helped ensure the success of so many of these trips in ways very few will ever know. He was like our "Angel in the Outfield" and could always be counted on to assist in any way needed. He never wanted the credit or accolades, but rather rejoiced in seeing the lasting impact that these trips had on the young people who took part in them. Even when he could not always personally attend, he would be the last to see us off and wish us blessings on the trip and the first to welcome us back, usually with a dinner.

- Br. Brian Poulin, one of the current Vocation Director for our USA Province, has always been greatly committed to offering his time and energy around Marist projects that allow young people an opportunity to make a significant difference, especially in the area of mission trips when we can dedicate ourselves to assisting persons in need in some of the poorest areas of our country and world.

John and Marcus Allen

Br. Owen and
Tomas O'Riordan working
hard

The A Team planning a
project over our annual
dinner

"We showed that we are united and that we, young people, are unstoppable."

– *Greta Thunberg*

# 22

## Two Crazy Guys

When I moved to West Virginia in the summer of 1998, I didn't realize that two former members of my campus ministry teams at Molloy would have such a profound effect on my years of ministry in West Virginia and ultimately on the rest of my life. When I began my time in Wheeling, there were incredible needs and very little resources to call upon for help. Br. Dave Cooney, one of the Brothers with whom I lived, and two Marist Sisters, Constance and Theresa, ran the 18th street homeless center. Br. Tom Kelly and I began our work at Bishop Donahue High School and every day was a new adventure at the school as there were many difficulties in those early days of our work there.

Dan Hurley was one of my original campus ministers when I began the program at Molloy. Nick "Chachi" Rella had just graduated from Molloy and was one of my campus ministers that year. He was heading off to college as I moved to the Mountain State. Both of them had accomplished many great works in our time together at Molloy, especially in running retreats and in our many efforts to support the homeless.

I came back to New York for Christmas and got together during the break with both Dan and Chachi. I shared many stories of West Virginia and some of the challenges we faced. Dan asked if he could bring a group of volunteers down from his college for their spring break. I said we would be grateful for any help they might be able to offer. Chachi said he would also take off that week and join the trip.

Somewhere around St. Patrick's Day our first volunteer group arrived from Plattsburgh State University led by Dan and with Chachi as a sidekick. During that week, the students were divided into three work groups. One group built all new shelves at the 18th Street Homeless Center, which feeds about three hundred homeless folks each day. The shelves would make an incredible difference to the Center. They were able to store all the non-perishable foods such as canned goods. The Center received a large tractor trailer supply of government issued canned goods about every six weeks. Those cans would help feed three hundred people six days a week. It took a lot of shelving to accommodate all the space that was needed. Twenty-two years later, those same shelves are still going strong and continue to help meet a great need. A second group of students helped refurbish our school gymnasium. All the ceiling tiles had been destroyed during the opening week of school after part of the roof collapsed into the gym. We managed to get the roofed fixed but needed much work to restore the gym to one that was respectable. All of the windows also needed to be replaced. Dan and his group were able to get both gym projects completed during that week.

The third and final group probably had the most profound effect of all. They ran one day retreats for each of the four classes. They gave all the talks and ran the small groups. As a result of those retreats our school's campus ministry program really took off. Students from the school also wanted to volunteer to work with the New York gang in helping to make the needed repairs in the gym. Each night the group gathered for an evening reflection and sharing which were sacred moments. Our school community and the 18th Street Center were beyond grateful for all the help and hosted a little dinner on their last night. The group then presented us with checks to help cover the cost of all the materials we needed for the projects. They had done fundraising for the past few months to raise enough to not only cover their costs but make these considerable and most generous donations. Dan, Chachi and other groups of college students from Plattsburgh returned each of the next five years and likewise made amazing impacts on our community. Dan and a few other of his volunteers also spent an entire summer living in my classroom so they could assist us during a major renovation of the school in the summer of 2001.

During the summers, I also brought groups of students from Bishop Donahue to work at four of the summer camps at the MBCE. Dan and Chachi also volunteered there during those summers and again had a great impact on our kids. I brought students up to Esopus to attend Marist Encounter retreats as well as to the Marist Youth Gatherings each May. These experiences profoundly influenced the spirit of our school as our students began to see a brand new world with many possibilities and opportunities.

Dan and Chachi both met amazing girlfriends whom they would both eventually marry. Dan actually came to know Cathy on that first service trip to West Virginia as she was one of the students from Plattsburgh who signed up for the week. Chachi brought his girlfriend Angela on one of the later service weeks as well. As the years moved on, we all continued to grow closer. Dan and Cathy have three amazing kids in Thomas, Matthew and Megan. Chachi and Angela likewise have great kids, named Allie, Anthony and Nicole. My life is incredibly blessed as I get to see those crazy rugrats every chance I can and those are always some of my best days. We all traveled to Italy together last summer and had one of the best vacations of our lives. We try to find frequent opportunities and ways to connect. Recently Dan, Cathy and the Hurley kids joined a week-long service trip I hosted in Esopus. The kids were inspiring and loved their first service experience. Hopefully they can continue to follow in the footsteps of their parents in how they respond to serving those in our world in need.

I am most proud of these two crazy guys not only because they have supported me since they were kids in high school in more ways than I could ever remember, but most of all because of the incredible husbands and fathers they have become. Their families and their faith are the two most important priorities in their lives and it clearly shows as both are raising three of the most beautiful and loving children God has ever created.

In Italy with Chachi, Dan and their families

# Final Thoughts

As I close this book, I hope and pray that many more young people, like the ones I shared about in these pages, will have the needed courage and faith to be the change that is required to make our world a better and more loving place. If one wants to change the world, it simply must be done one person at a time. I have yet to meet a young person that does not have the potential to do great things with their lives. Sometimes they just need to be given the chance. They also may require a little encouragement or an opportunity to realize what they are capable of accomplishing.

In the past thirty years, I have coordinated more than one hundred service mission trips and have seen young people work harder than anyone would ever believe and in every kind of difficult weather condition. I have watched thousands of counselors at the MBCE camps perform works of mercy for almost forty years. In all of those experiences there are two common factors about every one of those young people who carried out all those often very difficult tasks. The first is no one, not even a single one of these young people, ever complained about what they were asked to do. Secondly everything they were asked to do; they did with great love!

The needs of our world have never been greater than they are today, but we must not lose hope. I believe that our young people will lead the way to a brighter future. So many of them are far beyond previous generations in regard to their acceptance of others, caring about our common home, seeing diversity as a strength and most of all yearning for spirituality and God in their lives. Some of our young people today dance to a different drum than we older folks, may have at their age. But maybe it's time we stop listening to our old music and allow new verses to be created by these artists of the future. Our young people will create an amazing symphony of hope, faith and love if we allow them the opportunities to dance and sing their song for our world. Believe in them, pray for them, support them and watch miracles unfold as they help change our world.

# About the Author

Br. Dan O'Riordan, FMS, a Marist Brother, and currently Vice Provincial for the USA Province shares his inspiring stories of young people who have made significant impacts on the lives of many in our world in this, his second book. He graduated from Archbishop Molloy High School in New York, University College Cork, Ireland and earned an MA at Marist College in Poughkeepsie, NY.

He has served as a teacher, coach, counselor and campus minister at numerous Marist High Schools around the USA. He also served his Province as their Vocation Director.

He has coordinated more than one hundred mission service trips allowing many young people the opportunity to serve the least favored in many communities. He has also led numerous pilgrimages for young people and continues to be a featured speaker on youth retreats and youth gatherings, where he encourages young people to find ways to answer God's call and use their gifts and talents in responding to the many needs of our world.

www.brdanbooks.com

# Other Books by Br. Dan O'Riordan

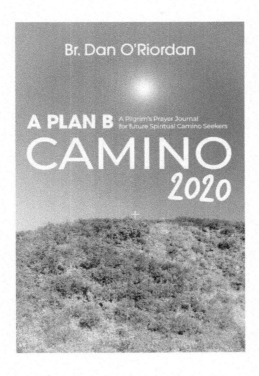

A Plan B Camino 2020: A Pilgrim's Prayer Journal for Future Spiritual Camino Seekers. Available in paperback or Kindle edition on Amazon.com

12.01.2020 1647